Buen Camin

My Camino

by

John Cowell

Vaya con Dios!

John Cowell

RB
Rossendale Books

Published by Lulu Enterprises Inc
3101 Hillsborough Street
Suite 2010
Raleigh NC 27607 – 5436
United States of America

Published in paperback 2015
Category: Travel Journal & Memoirs
Copyright © John Cowell 2015

ISBN 978-1-326-29353-6

Books by John Cowell

Non-Fiction

The Broken Biscuit

Cracks in the Ceiling

Elephant Grass

An American Journey

Poetry

My Life in Verse

Poems of Life

Foreword

Archbishop Oscar Romero is CAFOD's figurehead and the main office, "ROMERO HOUSE" in London is named after him. On 24th March 1980 Archbishop Oscar Romero of San Salvador was assassinated as he celebrated Mass. Because of his courageous stand for justice, he had already become a symbol of hope, strength and solidarity for those living in poverty in El Salvador. After his murder, Romero became a martyr for people struggling to break free from poverty and oppression throughout the world. He was a close friend of CAFOD, a man whom they honoured by including him in their address. He was an inspiration and his legacy continues. The following is a quote by the man himself:

"All pomp, all triumphs, all selfish capitalisma and all false successes of life will pass with the world's form. All falsehoods pass away, what does not pass away is love. When one turns money, property and work into a calling for the service of others, then the joy of sharing and the feeling that all are one family does not pass away. In the evening of one's life you will be judged on love".

Introduction

El Camino de Santiago de Compostela is a pilgrimage in Northern Spain that has been ongoing since the ninth century. It actually dates back even further to the era of Jesus Christ. Santiago translates to Saint James and a legend describes how, over two thousand years ago, Christians brought his remains back to Galicia and buried them in a field near to a large flowing river. After saying prayers for the dead the Christians departed from the site. The tomb was lost for many centuries but was discovered again in the ninth century by the bishop of Santiago. From that moment on many pilgrims visited the site and a magnificent cathedral, which still exists today, was built. Millions of pilgrims made their way from many countries. This continued right up to the 16th Century, but was disrupted when the famous English pirate, Francis Drake, attacked La Coruna. The tomb was lost for nearly three centuries but when it was discovered again the Pope declared it was indeed the authentic remains of Saint James. Once again pilgrims started to flow into Santiago and it is still ongoing and as popular today as it was ages ago. El Camino Frances is a route that starts in a little French village called San Juan Pie de Port at the foot of the Pyrenees Mountains. To reach Santiago pilgrims traipse well over 500 miles over rocky, mountainous terrain; and their only guide in the open wilderness are little yellow arrows painted on rocks and stones. Over the years many hopefuls have collapsed and died along the Holy Way. Proof of this are the many monuments and memorials dedicated to their memory. Indeed it is no easy task; pilgrims suffer from fatigue, dehydration, infected toenails, sore knees, painful backs and other debilitating injuries. So what is the reason for its popularity; why does it attract millions of pilgrims year after year? This is a question that has been asked many times and the answer is always the same. There's a spiritual feeling along the Camino that is unexplainable. As many pilgrims put it, "It is too hard to put into words." Many say they enjoy the journey because they connect to the energy of the masses who have walked the Camino before them. No matter the reason, most said they experienced an unexplainable spiritual feeling and felt they had tapped into something extra special. An average day's walk across rocky terrain is about 18 miles and to complete the total Camino takes about 30 days. What do these pilgrims gain by trekking arduously in all weathers with about 20 pounds on their back across flatlands and stony mountainous terrain? Many say it is to be pardoned of their sins; others that it is a way of being free from the many stressful things of life. But almost everyone agreed that the friendliness of their fellow pilgrims was exhilarating as they all came together on a spiritual path. Ultimately the Camino has a calling of its own and that is enough for many.

The Four Stages

According to folklore the Camino is divided into four stages:

1. BIRTH - SAN-JUAN-PIE de-PORT to PAMPLONA:
So called because it brings people together from all over the world in a spiritual way.

2. LIFE - PAMPLONA to BURGOS:
It makes one aware of the beauty of living together in complete spiritual happiness.

3. DEATH - BURGOS to LEON:
Thought to be so called because of the flat wide open wilderness with hardly any shade. As flatland stretches mile after mile in front of the pilgrims, together with inclement weather, every ache and pain appears to become exaggerated.

4. REBIRTH - LEON to SANTIAGO:
On reaching Santiago pilgrims gather their thoughts together and ask themselves what they have gained from trekking countless miles over hostile wilderness. Most reach the conclusion that it frees them from the hectic pace of everyday living and that it gives them a feeling of complete satisfaction.

Contents

Foreword
Introduction
The Four Stages

Chapters

The Way 1
Learning Spanish 10
Our Pilgrim Friend 19
The Camino 26

Photos 54-86

Chapters (continued)

The Street Children of Brazil 87
Santiago de Compostela 107
Camino Guides 147
Appendix 181

MY CAMINO AMIGO

Chapter One

The Way

Here I was on a train heading for London with my friend, Fred Uttley. We were going to the capital to attend a meeting regarding a famous pilgrimage in Northern Spain. Fred, a keen hardworking volunteer for 'CAFOD' (CATHOLIC AGENCY FOR OVERSEAS DEVELOPMENT), a world wide charity organisation, had been called upon to act as a guide, along with me, for fourteen would be pilgrims. This stemmed from the fact that Fred and I had walked the Camino several times in an effort to raise money for under privileged countries throughout the world. After alighting from the train we made our way via the underground to Romero House, the charity's headquarters, where we met up with our future travelling companions.

Our planned pilgrimage was to take place in six weeks' time and taking on the project was no easy task. The group consisted of men and women whose ages ranged from early twenties to late sixties.

During the meeting Fred discussed the ups and downs of the strenuous journey and made it clear that it wouldn't be like a stroll in the park. "I must point out," he stressed, "that the only guide for the majority of pilgrims are little yellow arrows which mark the way. These are little markers painted on rocks and stones at various points where the path divides into two. You need to be vigilant, especially in mountainous country, or you could find yourself in serious trouble. In your case you'll have John and me to fall back on, but you mustn't take things for granted." He paused for a minute before going back into serious vein, "Another thing that you must do when you go home from here, you must prepare yourself well in advance before you attempt this challenge. If you get blisters on the walk then your pilgrimage is finished. The only way to avoid this is by walking a few miles every day to harden the soles of your feet. Don't overdo it at first, let's say two to three miles a day, and gradually build it up to ten miles. Try practicing with a rucksack on your back as you'll have to carry at least twelve kilos on the Camino. On the pilgrimage it is advisable to bring a sleeping bag, a walking staff, a flashlight and a penknife with you. Also it is essential that you wear a hat to protect you from the sun."

After a few more basic instructions he then quoted some facts and a little history about the pilgrimage:

El Camino de Santiago de Compostela is a pilgrimage in Northern Spain that has been ongoing since the ninth century. Pilgrims from all over the world travel to Spain to make the arduous journey. Many do it to rejuvenate themselves spiritually whereas many others do it simply as a challenge. Others do it solely to obtain a 'COMPOSTELA'. This is a certificate to say they have made the strenuous journey. Whatever the reason, most pilgrims find it a very enlightening experience as many things unfold during their magical journey. Even non-believers are touched by the unexplainable feelings they experience along the Holy Way. There are many routes that can be undertaken, but the most popular one is 'El Camino Frances'. This route commences in a small French village, 'San Juan Pie de Port', at the foot of the Pyrenees Mountains, a distance of over eight hundred kilometers from Santiago. To walk the entire distance it takes about a month covering approximately eighteen miles a day. This is no easy task taking into consideration that each pilgrim has to carry a rucksack weighing around twelve kilograms. Other factors to be considered are weather conditions, fatigue, blisters and a need for a steady water supply. For example, the first day's walk is a strenuous fourteen-mile steep uphill climb to the peak of the Pyrenees and then a long downhill grind into Roncesvalles, a Spanish village. Before the taxing journey commences each pilgrim has to obtain credentials from an 'albergue'. An albergue is the Spanish name for a hostel. The credential is a type of passport which allows a pilgrim to stay in one of the many albergues along the way to Santiago. A person does not have to commence his journey from San Juan Pie de Port; he may start it from any town along the way so long as he obtains a passport. But to obtain a COMPOSTELA CERTIFICATE a pilgrim has to walk at least the last hundred kilometers to Compostela.

El Camino de Santiago translates to 'The Way of St James', and Compostela means 'Field of the Star'. According to legend, over 2000 years ago in the era of Jesus Christ, a small group of Christians arrived in a small boat on the coast of Galicia and brought with them a coffin containing the remains of Saint James. They sailed up the river Ulla to a region ruled by Queen Lupa, and after listening to their story she gave the Christians a yoke of oxen to help them carry the coffin. They gradually reached a suitable spot and buried the remains in a field by the side of the river. After saying prayers for his soul the Christians departed from the scene. Centuries passed by and nothing more was heard about it until something rare occurred in the Ninth Century. The bishop of Santiago noticed brilliant lights shining up from a field by the river Ulla and also bright lights were shining downwards from a shining star. These separate lights intertwined and formed a dazzling beam. The bishop ordered peasants to excavate the field and within a short spell they discovered a massive underground tomb. After a lot of deliberation the bishop proclaimed that they had uncovered the tomb of St James. Word spread around quickly and before long thousands of pilgrims from far and wide visited the burial ground. Miracles began to take place; blind people realised they could see, deaf people could hear and crippled people began to walk again. The news spread further afield and pilgrims started to emerge onto the place from far away countries. A small church was built and in the first year over a million pilgrims made their way over countless miles of treacherous wilderness. This was a tedious task taking into account that once they'd reached Santiago, they then had to walk all the way back to their homeland. Two hundred years passed and in the eleventh century a magnificent cathedral was built. Also along the different routes, many monasteries and albergues were built where pilgrims could pass the night. In the same century a French monk, Almiera Picaud, wrote the first guidebook for tourists.

More time passed by and in the year 1589 a renowned English pirate, Francis Drake, attacked La Coruna in Northern Spain and, in desperation, the bishop of Santiago hid the remains of St James.

Three centuries passed by and nobody knew their whereabouts, but then in the 19th Century they were discovered again. This time the Pope intervened and after deep consideration he declared that they were indeed the remains of St James. On this occasion the sacred remains were placed into a casket and laid to rest within the Cathedral. Once again many pilgrims emerged onto the city to visit the site.

Today in the 21st Century, over two million pilgrims visit Santiago every year and they stay overnight in one of the many albergues built along the way.

In the Middle Ages the burial site was called in Latin, 'Campus Stella', meaning Field of the Star. But with the passing of time the name gradually changed to Compostela.

Fred paused for a little and then added another rather interesting fact. *In the Middle Ages if a convict committed a serious offence which warranted a five year jail sentence he was given a choice. He could either serve his sentence or walk the entire Camino from San Juan Pie de Port and back again. This may come across to you as*

an easy option, but the snag was he had to do it wearing handcuffs
and steel shackles on his ankles.

After finishing his little speech Fred asked the class for any questions.

"Excuse me, I have one" said Pat Downs, a Guilford lady who was a little apprehensive after listening to the tale. "Are there any instances of pilgrims being attacked and robbed whilst roaming in the mountain wilderness?"

"Good question Pat because in the Middle Ages that was certainly the case. There were many cases back then when people left their homeland never to return as they were plundered and murdered along the Way. However, over a hundred years ago, the Spanish Parliament put strict laws in place which now protect and safeguard the many pilgrims along the Way."

"And do you get many women walking the Camino?"

"Yes you do Pat and surprisingly many young girls from many countries do it all on their own. I was very surprised when I first noticed this and so I walked along with odd ones and asked them if they felt afraid at all. Their answer was always the same."

"And what was that?"

"'Oh I did feel rather apprehensive at the very start,' each one would reply, 'but on the Way, even in the wilderness, I felt quite safe. There's a special feeling in the atmosphere, it's a spiritual feeling that's hard to explain but there it is. Mind you, every pilgrim along the Camino is so helpful and friendly, and this really helped me to feel at ease.'"

After the formalities Fred and I socialised with the group in an effort to get to know each other a little better. One of them was Tony McNichols a Welsh man. Another was John Fogarty from London and both men were really keen and excited about walking the Camino.

As Fred and I made our way back home on the train we talked about the Camino and how our present situation had come about. We both agreed that the task before us was not going to be an easy one by any means.

Chapter Two

Learning Spanish

Whilst on holiday in Tenerife over thirty years ago I noticed how people from Germany, Holland, Belgium, Italy and other places could all speak English. On the other hand, neither I, nor any other Englishman there could speak another language. This got me to thinking how lazy we English people are. It also made me determined to learn Spanish and so, as soon as I got back home, I booked into night school classes.

It was in this class that I met Fred and it became obvious that he was as keen to learn Spanish as I was. Our Spanish teacher, a young lady called Margaret Walsh, was very proficient and made the lessons very interesting. So much so that Fred and I actually went to her house once a week for private tuition. We both did well in the basic Spanish class and our teacher encouraged us to upgrade to GCSE studies. Our enthusiasm grew and we both progressed into the A-level class. The format was now much harder but, with encouragement from our former teacher and sheer determination, we both got grades to take us on to University and apply for a degree course.

I was rather reluctant at first, but Fred encouraged me, "Come on John, we can do it. We've come this far; we may as well go the whole hog."

"That's all very well Fred, but what about all the homework we'll get and the extra studying. And don't forget, it's a five-year course."

"Yeah I've thought about that but what have we got to lose. Even if we don't make the grade, our Spanish is bound to improve."

"Aye alright Fred, you've got a good point there; I never thought of it that way ... I'll do it! Anyway, while we're on the subject of improving our Spanish, how about spending some time in Spain?"

"Yeah I'll go along with that, I can't see a better way of putting our Spanish into practice."

So we did go to Spain a few times and our learning came on leaps and bounds which paid dividends in the classroom. Whilst in Spain we took the opportunity to talk to each other in Spanish and we addressed each other using our Spanish names – Federico and Juanito. It was during our first year at Preston University that fate took a hand in our destiny. We had lots of written and reading tests to do which were by no means easy. But then came an oral test which was rather nerve racking. We had to stand up in front of the classroom and speak in Spanish for ten minutes. But one thing that made it easier was that we could speak about any topic.

"Bloomin' 'eck Fred," I moaned, "it's hard enough to give a speech for ten minutes in English, never mind in Spanish."

"Aye, I know what you mean John. But at least we can talk about anything we want to."

It was then that an idea came to me. "I know what I'm going to do Fred."

"Oh Yeah, and what's that then?"

"I'm going to borrow a few Spanish books from the library and read up on different legends about Spain."

"That's a good idea John because I think every little town or village throughout Spain has its own special legend."

He was right too. The Spanish people seem to excel in creating legends about their own village or hamlet, no matter how small it is. One legend that I found very interesting was about an aqueduct in Segovia. It had been built by the Romans over two thousand years ago and the Segovian people nicknamed it 'El Obra del Diablo,' meaning 'The Bridge of the Devil'. I found other interesting ones, but then I came across 'El Camino de Santiago de Compostela' and this really fired up my imagination. I couldn't wait to show it Fred and he became as engrossed as I was.

"I'll tell you what John; I'd love to do a pilgrimage to Santiago," he enthused, "it sounds really interesting."

"Yeah so would I … we'll have to give it a go first chance we get."

We were both keen on the idea of walking the Camino but, as we both had busy schedules, we tended to let it pass by. Besides, my wife was ill with kidney failure and had to attend hospital three times a week for dialysis.

Also Fred was a keen volunteer for CAFOD and he spent many hours every week visiting various schools in order to talk to children and make them aware of the poverty in many poor countries throughout the world. On occasions he'd call upon me to give him a hand and it was good to watch him at work. He'd use props to help him with his talks; for example he'd carry a bucket of murky water into the classroom. He narrated tales of how African children have to walk miles to collect water from dirty rivers polluted with animal waste and then carry it back to their village in pails. He then dipped a glass tumbler into the bucket and asked the class, "Would anyone like a drink?"

The response was a loud refusal throughout the classroom, "U-ug-gh no!!"

Other times he'd arrange organ recitals in various cathedrals which involved a lot of work with seating arrangements and other things. Fun days and cross country running around local parks was

14

another of his specialties and he'd call upon volunteers to help erect tents and tables. He asked each volunteer to wear a yellow CAFOD vest and act as stewards to the gathering crowd and contestants alike. Fred undertook all these events and many more to raise lots of money for well-deserving causes. Another major effort he did was to go to war-torn Liberia, in Africa with a few others to set up the building of a school and a water well. He donated a complete set of football strips to encourage youngsters in that war-torn area to participate in sport and other activities. The event touched Fred very much as youngsters, only ten years old, were being versed in the art of war and how to use weapons. The poor little tots actually walked about carrying guns.

This man certainly impressed me with his kindness and willingness to give up his free time for others. And this is why I was always ready and willing to help him when he called upon my services. I felt privileged and honoured to be helping this gentleman. There was another reason why I supported his cause and that was because my mother had done charity work from her home for the last thirty years of her life. Over that period she raised lots of money for deserving causes, especially when natural disasters had taken place throughout the world. And her favourite charity was CAFOD.

Sadly, not all charities are genuine. In fact, it has come to light that some are downright unscrupulous and tend to scoop the cream off all monies donated to them. Luckily most wayward charities have been brought to task and strict laws are now in place. Still, the damage has been done and now many people condemn all charities alike and refuse to give anything.

Fred's reason for supporting CAFOD so devoutly was simple and to the point as I found out one day as we discussed various charities. "I support CAFOD John," he said, "because I trust them implicitly. There are rumours that some charities are getting rich from the proceeds and that's why many people won't donate anything. And in some ways you can't blame them because they tarnish all charities with the same brush"

"I know what you mean Fred because my mother had the same problem. When she was trying to collect charity money people would often say to her, 'Why should I give to charity just to make some rich man even richer. And anyway, I think that only a pittance of the money gets through to where it's supposed to'. My mum's answer to that was that if people didn't give anything then poor impoverished people throughout the world would get nothing at all."

"That may well be," said Fred, "but I've researched into CAFOD and they only take about eight percent out of donations for administration costs. And they guarantee that over ninety percent of all monies gets through to many deserving causes throughout the world. Because of this I've set up a special organisation in my own parish and it's called, OUT REACH TO THE WORLD."

Fred's enthusiasm and devotion to helping his fellow man in distressing conditions rubbed off on me and I felt strongly that I needed to help him in his good work. And so it came to pass that he called upon me on a regular basis and I began to realise why he was so devout in his intentions. Every time I gave some of my time to help in one of his causes it gave me a feeling of complete satisfaction. It's hard to put into words how I felt, but it's a feeling that makes life feel worthwhile.

This was the pattern of things and then came a very low point in my life … my wife died. I sank to a very low point and couldn't concentrate on anything. After the funeral I told Fred that I was giving up my studying at university as I felt too traumatised. Being the friend he was he gave it up too.

"Not to worry Juan, we can always pick it up again later."

He was a good mate and after a short while I continued to help him carry out his good work. It actually helped me to cope with my grief.

Chapter Three

Our Pilgrim Friend

In between charity work Fred and I took ourselves off to Spain to practice our Spanish. On one occasion we spent a week in Madrid and once again, fate took a hand in our lives. It was a bright summer's evening and we were in a bar having tapas when a fellow traveller came in wearing boots and shorts with a rucksack on his back. He happened to stand next to us at the bar and appeared to be overjoyed and full of excitement.

Fred noticed the stranger's happy attitude and introduced himself. "Good evening sir, you must have had a good day; you appear to be in high spirits."

"You can say that again," replied the man with a big smile on his face, "I've just spent the most wonderful two weeks of my life."

"Oh, you've been on holiday have you?"

"Well I suppose you could say that because I am on leave from work. But where I've been has been more exhilarating than any holiday I've ever been on in my life before."

By now my curiosity was aroused and so I joined in the conversation. "And where would that be my friend, it seems to be very exciting?"

His answer completely floored Fred and me and it wasn't just what he told us. As he narrated his escapade his whole countenance seemed to light up with enthusiasm. "You may not have heard about it my friends but I have just done two week's pilgrimage in Northern Spain on The Way of St James."

"Oh you don't mean El Camino de Santiago de Compostela?" both Fred and I asked eagerly.

"That's the very same one," he replied with a smile on his face.

This man, who had just come into our lives, had Fred and me all fired up. "Oh come on mate" said Fred excitably, "you've got to tell us what it's like, we've been thinking about doing the pilgrimage ourselves for ages."

As he spoke his whole being appeared vibrant and alive and his eyes seemed to sparkle with happiness. "Well where do I start?" said the over-excited fellow traveller. "So many things happened in such a short time. First of all along the Way there are many albergues where you can stay for the night and they're completely run by volunteers. I stayed at several on my travels and each one greeted me with the utmost courtesy and treated me like royalty. The hostels are very basic just like an army barrack room but the atmosphere of the place welcomed me with open arms. In some of them there are as many as eighty beds, including bunk beds. Men and women all sleep in the same room and share cold water showers. This may seem strange, but yet it works out fine as every pilgrim is extremely polite and discreet and respects each other's privacy. The average cost is just five hundred pesetas a night, about three pounds, and you get bed and breakfast for that. You have to be in bed for ten o'clock every night and they get you up early next morning at six o'clock. I enjoyed this aspect of it because after walking about eighteen miles a day I was exhausted and really looked forward to my bed. As for getting up at six o'clock, that was good as well because it gave me a chance to do most of my walking before the sun got too hot. As I walked along the Way I made many friends of people from all over the world. I can't even begin to explain the wonderful atmosphere of the Camino and how it makes you feel. It's a feeling out of this world and all I can say is you have to do it yourself to experience it. I cannot possibly put it into words."

"Just one more thing," asked Fred, "if you come across a V junction up in the mountains, how do you know which path to take?"

"Good question mate. Well when this happens you will always find a little yellow arrow pointing you in the right direction. It's a simple idea but believe me it's very effective."

"Little yellow arrows," Fred laughed. "I'm certainly looking forward to seeing them."

Fred and I could not believe our luck ...we were talking to someone who had actually walked the Camino. The sheer happiness and vibrancy bouncing off this man had a definite effect on Fred and me.

In our excited state something rather funny happened. It wasn't funny for the poor bloke at the time, but even he joined in afterwards and had a laugh about it. It turned out that after finishing his pilgrimage the poor man was almost skint.

"Would you like a drink with us to celebrate the occasion?" said Fred.

"No, it's alright," replied the gentleman, "I wouldn't be able to buy you one back as I've just enough money left to get me to the airport tomorrow."

"That's alright my Camino friend," said Fred, "have a few drinks on John and me. After what you've just told us, you deserve it."

Well the man did join us and he thoroughly enjoyed himself as we celebrated his achievement over the next hour. When we bade him goodbye he still had half a beer left in his glass.

What caused the problem for the traveller was that Fred and I had frequented the same bar every night and the staff had permitted us to buy our drinks on tab. Before we left each evening we settled the outstanding bill. However, on this occasion we were so engrossed with the stranger's tale that we actually left the bar without settling our account and didn't realise it until we'd arrived back at our digs.

"Oh no!" blurted Fred. "We've walked out of that bar without paying the bill!"

"Oh 'eck, that poor bloke will be panicking," I said realising his predicament, "he'll think he's been conned."

"Come on John, we'd best get back there quick and sort it out, the poor bloke will be doing his nut."

Well we arrived back at the bar about ten minutes later and, sure enough, our stranger friend was in a right state. But his anxiety changed somewhat when he saw us.

"Oh thank goodness you've come back … they were just about to call the police and have me thrown in nick because I couldn't pay the bill."

"Oh well never mind eh!" laughed Fred. "All's well that ends well."

"I'll go along with that," chuckled the stranger, "for a horrible moment I thought I'd been conned."

"We thought that you may be thinking that," said Fred, "that's why we rushed back here."

"I couldn't believe what was happening to me," smiled the man, "`especially after my wonderful feeling on the Camino amongst so many beautiful people."

"A wonderful feeling," said Fred curiously, "how do you mean?"

"I'm sorry mate, like I said before; I can't possibly describe it in words; to experience the feeling of the Camino you've got to walk it yourself."

Well that was it! On our way back to our digs Fred and I decided that our next trip out to Spain would be to undertake the pilgrimage.

Chapter Four

The Camino

Our determination remained and our next trip out to Spain was to walk on the blessed route. We weren't sure where to start our Camino from and decided to fly to Barcelona. After making enquiries we then had to catch a bus to Pamplona, a distance of over 150 miles. To our surprise we were informed that the Spanish let bulls run through the streets of this little town prior to entering the bullring. Local youths run in front of the bulls and jump over barriers or onto window ledges. Only days previously an American had attempted it and was gored to death.

We went to a tourist information office and obtained a map of our route and it was there we were informed that we had to obtain a passport in order to stay in various albergues.

"Well John," said Fred after looking at the map, "our first day's walk is to 'Puente la Reina,' a little village about twenty six kilometers from here."

"Oh I've read about that Federico, it's a famous monument known as 'Bridge of the Queen'. How far is it from here in miles?"

"Let's see," he said putting his thinking cap on," eight kilometers is equal to five miles. So according to my reckoning it's about sixteen miles."

That shouldn't be too bad, I thought, because we'd done a lot of walking back in England. But then I was in for a bit of a shock as I discovered after opening my rucksack. "Oh no Fred, I don't believe it!"

"What's up mate ... what don't you believe?"

"Well you know all that walking that we've done before coming here?"

"Yeah, what about it?"

"Well you're not going to believe this," I repeated, "but I've gone and left my boots back home and the only shoes I have with me are soft leather ones."

Consequently, I had to set off early next morning without any boots.

"Never mind Fred, I'll put up with these for now," I said living in hope. "Maybe we'll come across a shop in a village along the route where I can buy some boots."

It turned out there was little chance of that. As we approached the outskirts of the small town we were confronted with a long winding mountain road which stretched miles in front of us into wide open country. As we climbed steadily we were rewarded with idyllic panoramic views. Our path was gritty but to either side of us were large fields of corn that swayed in the wind like the waves on an ocean. Beyond the fields, as far as the eye could see, were beautiful meandering mountains. Way in front of us we could see windmills sat on the top of other outlying mountains.

"I'll tell you what John," said Fred taking in a deep breath of nature's fresh air, "the views from up here are stunning, take a look at all the different colours on that mountain range."

"You're right there Fred, it takes your breath away doesn't it?"

"Aye you're right there, and so does this here climb," he joked. "And we're not even half way up this mountain yet. Just look at

28

those windmills up yonder in the distance, they look like match-sticks from here."

During our steady climb, many fast walkers passed us and, likewise, we passed many pilgrims who were slower walkers than us. We soon discovered that every person along the Way was very friendly and helpful and each one greeted us with the words, "Buen Camino!"

Our thoughts went out to two Canadian ladies, Polly and Eileen, who appeared to be struggling. Fred had a word with them but they were not overly concerned.

"Are you sure," asked Fred, "I don't like the thought of leaving you alone on this mountain?"

"Thanks a lot for your concern," smiled Polly, "but I can assure you we'll be alright, we do a lot of rambling back home in Ontario."

"Yeah," laughed Eileen, "it's just that we're out of puff climbing up this mountain."

"Right fair enough girls, we'll be on our way then."

As we progressed up the mountain we came across different paths but our way was always guided by a little yellow arrow as we had been forewarned. We plodded on and it took Fred and me about three hours to reach the peak but it was well worth it. The view was now out of this world as beautiful vistas greeted us from every direction. We rested for a while and replenished ourselves with dry bread and jam and swilled it down with fresh water from a fountain. It may seem strange, but the bread and jam tasted like nectar. It was during this respite that we met up with an American guy called Matthew.

"Oh that was my grandfather's name," I said introducing myself, "but everybody used to call him Mat."

"Yeah, that's what I get called back in Arizona too," he answered with a smile.

"And what made you come all this way from America to walk the Camino?" I asked.

"Oh, it's something I read about years ago and I found it so fascinating that I've wanted to do it ever since."

"And are you walking all the way to Santiago?"

"Well let's put it this way, that's my intention. Whether I make it is another thing."

I knew what he meant because he was a very large overweight gentleman, weighing around twenty stone and appeared rather unfit. "U-um," I mumbled to myself, "if he can make it I should be able to."

Now came the second leg of our journey and it was an extremely steep descent through a narrow gorge. We'd been warned about this by a local Pamplona man.

"Cuidate! La Montana es muy peligrosa con muchas pierdras y rocas," he'd stressed.

He actually warned us to take care as the descent was very steep and dangerous with lots of hazardous stones and rocks.

"He wasn't kidding Federico," I moaned as I kept slipping onto my back, "I can feel every little pebble with every step I take."

"Yeah, and be careful of those bigger rocks Juanito, they're real ankle breakers."

31

It was during this strenuous downhill haul that I noticed that many pilgrims had walking poles to assist them. I certainly could have done with one as it would have taken a lot of pressure off my knees. By the time we reached the bottom of the gorge two more hours had passed by. We took another rest and then began the third leg of our journey. The going was a lot flatter and much easier, but we'd only covered a third of our journey. We'd still fifteen kilometers to go and my feet were feeling worse for wear. I struggled on but my mate encouraged me all the way. It was funny really because the two Canadian ladies actually overtook us.

"Come on gentlemen," joked Polly as she passed us, "we don't want to be late for supper ... Buen Camino!"

Along the route we passed through a little hamlet where small children were playing. I had to smile to myself as some of them started chuckling as we passed by them. With hands over their mouths the tiny tots sniggered and mocked us. "Eh, eh-eh—e-eh perigrinos!" chuckled bigger ones and other little ones reiterated the same chorus one after the other. Some of them followed us for a short while with their childish mocking tones. But they quickly dispersed when we turned around and pretended to be annoyed. Their little mischievous games actually perked me up and made me feel better. It took me back to my childhood when I had done similar things.

Hours passed by and we finally arrived at our first albergue around six o'clock that evening. It had been a hard trek and both Fred and I were ready for a rest and something to eat.

We booked into the refugio and our passport was stamped and dated with an official stamp. At the back of the building there was a large garden area with lots of clothes hanging on washing lines. It turned out that most of the pilgrims had arrived about three o'clock in the afternoon.

"It's very important that you arrive at your albergue as soon as possible to wash socks and underclothes," pointed out a friendly pilgrim. "If your clothes are not dry when you set off in the morning then you have to drape them on the outside of your rucksack."

"I know what he means Federico," I said, "if I don't take off these sweaty socks of mine, they'll crawl away."

"I know what he means too," laughed Fred, "mine are heaving too!"

After washing our socks and underpants we were ready for something to eat.

"Come along with us," said a friendly group who were just about to leave the albergue, "we're going for a 'menu del perigrino'." Amongst the group were Polly, Eileen and Matthew.

"Oh, a special menu for pilgrims," said Fred, "this sounds interesting."

We gladly accepted their invitation and they took us to a small inn. Once inside we all sat around a large table like one big happy family. "Look at this Juanito," said Fred showing me the menu, "we get a starter, a main meal, a dessert and a bottle of wine between the two of us."

"Great!" I responded. "And all for six euros."

Well the evening went well as we talked about the Camino and finished off with a sing-along.

"Right we'd best be heading back to the albergue, it's nearly ten o'clock," said one of them.

My mind went back to what our fellow traveller back in the Madrid bar had told Fred and me ... and he was right too, after a grueling walk on the Camino I was certainly ready for my bed. However, our first night in the albergue was very enlightening and brought brutal reality. Faced with poor washing facilities and cold showers it took all of my remaining energy to hoist myself into a top bunk. I didn't get much sleep at all because of all the snoring and other bodily sounds. When I finally managed to drop off I was awoken before dawn by beeping alarms, pilgrims unfastening zippers, the sound of crackling velcro and running water. Looking around the room pilgrims were packing their rucksacks in the dark by the aid of tiny torches.

Fred and I had little alternative but to join them and after a sparse breakfast we set off on our second day's journey at 6-30 am.

"How far have we to walk today?" I asked Fred.

"We're going to a place called Estella," he smiled, "and it's about the same distance as we walked yesterday."

My feet didn't seem too bad at first but as the miles progressed and the Way got stonier, blisters began to appear. The walk wasn't as hilly as our first day but after sixteen kilometers I was for giving up. But that was out of the question because we were way out in the wilderness. Fred encouraged me onwards but every step I took was sheer agony. Luckily we came across a fast-flowing river where I was able to soak my feet.

"Oh this is heaven Federico," I sighed with relief, "if we stay here for a while maybe I'll be able to make it."

"I've got to admit it looks inviting Juanito; I think I'll join you."

As we dangled our feet in the cool refreshing water we noticed an ancient stone humped back bridge with three arches spanning the river.

"I'll tell you what Juanito," said Fred, "I'm almost sure that's a Roman bridge."

"Yeah, I think you're right Federico, because those stone archways are typical of Roman architecture."

"Do you realise, we could be looking at something that is over two thousand years old?"

It truly was an historical work of art and we were both impressed by the magnificent structure.

After our short respite I told Fred that I was now ready to finish our journey. That's what I thought but when I put my shoes back on I could barely put my feet to the ground. And we still had ten kilometers to go.

"I'll tell you what Federico," I moaned, "if only I had something decent to wear on my feet I think I could make it. But as it is you'll have to leave me here."

"There's no chance of that," he replied, "we started this Camino together and we'll finish it together."

It was then that something very strange happened, a kind of miracle if you will. As Fred stood up he glanced across the river and saw some discarded rubbish on the other bank. We couldn't fathom out how it had got there out in the middle of nowhere.

"Just hang about here Juanito and I'll nip over the bridge to see what it is."

When he returned I couldn't believe what he was carrying.

"I don't know whether these will fit you Juanito," he smiled dangling a pair of sport's trainers in front of me, "I found them on top of a discarded bed mattress. They're a bit worn but they should be a lot better than those flimsy shoes you're wearing."

It turned out they were slightly too small but to counteract that I cut the upper part of the trainers around the toe area with a penknife.

"O-oh, these are great Federico; they must be heaven-sent." And I really meant it … how else could they have just appeared in this vast wilderness? When I stood up the thicker leather soles cushioned my feet and eased some of the pain. They weren't perfect but the deep leather soles protected my feet against the many sharp pebbles.

"Ha ha," laughed Fred, "you look really funny Jaunito! You're a true pilgrim now with your toes peeping out of those trainers; they look like open toe sandals."

"Eh Federico, you can laugh all you want. I don't care how funny I look; these trainers are a godsend. Come on mate, we've got some serious walking to do ... let's go!"

After crossing to the far side of the river we both looked at the rubbish lying there.

"How the flamin' 'eck has that rubbish got here?" I asked. "There are no roads or pathways around here?"

"Beats me," replied Fred, "perhaps an angelic creature left it here for you Juanito."

"Most people would laugh at that Federico, but have you got a better explanation?"

Fred had to admit that he hadn't. Well that was it; we were both amazed by this strange occurrence. But I was eternally grateful as we made our way to our second albergue. The trainers certainly helped and I lengthened my stride so as to put my heel down first and take some pressure off my soles. This worked to a point, but the damage had already been done. We got to within a kilometer of Estella and I had to stop again as the pain was excruciating. To add to my problem I wasn't wearing a hat and I was feeling very dehydrated.

I felt that I couldn't move another step but, once again, my mate encouraged me on. "Come on Juanito, only a little way to go now; you can make it."

I felt as though I was letting him down and this made me determined to carry on. So I literally dragged myself the last short stretch to the village. On the path we came across a memorial denoting that a pilgrim had collapsed and died on that very spot.

Oh 'eck! I thought … that poor soul didn't make it. Little did we know that we were going to come across many more memorials like this one on our travels. After saying a prayer for the departed it actually perked me up and spurred me on.

About two hundred yards from the albergue Polly came out to greet us and she had some bad news. "I'm sorry to tell you lads, the albergue is full but..."

In my anguished state I didn't let her finish, "Oh don't say that; I can't possibly walk another step. I'll just have to sleep out under the stars tonight!"

"It won't come to that," she said. "I was just going to tell you that they have some beds in an old stable."

"I'm not bothered about that," I grunted, "as long as there's a bed to park my body in, it'll do me."

The stable turned out to be a large barn with a flag floor and there were no washing or toilet facilities. For hygiene purposes we were allowed to use the albergue.

That evening, we once again enjoyed a special meal with our fellow travellers. Sat beside me at the table was a small Dutch lady called Elsina and, despite only being able to speak pigeon English, she was very friendly. When Fred and I got back to the stable Elsina happened to be in the bed next to me. "Shu-s-sh," she whispered as we fumbled about in the dark. Other pilgrims were fumbling too but they had flashlights to assist them.

"Blimey," commented Fred, "we never thought of bringing a flashlight did we?"

We soon discovered that we should have brought something else too.

We had a couple of blankets and a pillow each, but Elsina looked as cosy as a bug in a rug as she snuggled in between a sleeping bag. Looking around the barn I realised that everyone else had a sleeping bag too.

"It doesn't matter Federico," I said, "we'll be alright with these blankets."

"Yeah, I'm sure we will."

We couldn't have been more wrong. The inside of the barn was like an ice box. Within an hour I was absolutely chilled to the bone. "I can't believe this," I mumbled under the bed blankets, "this afternoon I was roasting to death and now I'm freezing my nuts off."

I tried sitting on the side of the bed with my arms wrapped around my shoulders but it didn't help. When I peered into the darkness Fred was doing the same whereas Elsina and the others were snoring away. It was a long night and was I glad when the early morning call was made.

"Oh thank goodness for that Federico!" I chattered through shivering lips.

"I know what you mean Juanito, I've never been as cold in my life."

"Aye me too, the only good thing about it was that it took my mind off my feet. Anyway, let's go and have a bit of breakfast before we hit the road."

Breakfast was served up by volunteers and afterwards, as I hobbled to the door a young lad approached me. "You seem to be struggling my friend," he said rather concerned as he handed me a hat. "Wear this sir because it's going to be very hot today and you may get sunstroke." He also gave me a small badge to fasten into the hat and told me it was a tradition for pilgrims to give each other emblems as a token of friendship. I was rather touched by his kind gesture.

Most pilgrims were making for Los Arcos, a distance of twenty-eight kilometers, and many had set off at 5am in the dark.

"I'll tell you what Juanito," said Fred after weighing up the situation, "let's take it easy today, we can stop in a little mountain village that's only nine kilometers from here."

"Great, I'll go along with that; it'll give my feet a chance to heal up."

My feet felt a little better but halfway to the village my blisters began to erupt again. But then I got further encouragement, Matthew, Polly, Eileen and Elsina were waiting for us by a water fountain.

"We've decided to walk along with you," said Polly acting as spokesperson for the group, "and we're all going to stop with you in the next village."

Spurred on by their friendship I struggled on and finally reached the hamlet three hours later. It was hard work but, just like our first day, we were amply rewarded by a beautiful landscape. The small village was sat high on a mountaintop and surrounded by rolling green fields. A gorgeous forest by the side of a dazzling blue lake gave the backdrop to this stunning vista. It was only mid afternoon and we all thoroughly enjoyed the idyllic surroundings and discussed the spiritual feeling of the Camino. Everyone came to the same conclusion that the Camino was a very special place. One thing made me laugh. Fred was sat on a wooden form and Matthew came and sat beside him. It's a pity I didn't have a camera because Fred looked like a little boy at the side of this enormous fellow. That evening after our meal we once again had a sing-along but on this occasion our voices all seemed to synchronise beautifully. Maybe it was because of the pure mountain air, but I truly think it was because of the beautiful ambience created by loving friendly people.

"How's your feet Juanito?" asked Fred as I hobbled to the dormitory.

"Just take a look," I replied raising my legs.

"Oh crikey!" he blurted. "The top layer of skin has completely disappeared; your feet look like two lumps of raw meat."

"Never mind Federico," I sighed, "let's see what tomorrow brings."

When I reached my bed Elsina was once again snuggled in a sleeping bag in the bed next to mine.

"U-umph," joked Fred as he snuggled beneath the bedclothes, "it looks like you've got an admirer Juanito."

Thankfully the dormitory was much warmer than the previous night and we both caught up on a good night's rest.

Morning arrived and more special things awaited me. After breakfast every other pilgrim got off to an early start. We'd nineteen kilometers to go to reach Los Arcos and I knew I'd to sort something out to give me any chance of making it. I had some very thick woollen socks in my rucksack and Fred came up with an idea.

"Juanito, why don't you put those thick socks halfway over the trainers and double the other half underneath you feet?"

"Seems a good idea Federico but how do I hold them in place?"

"Hang on a bit, I'll nip outside and see if I can find something."

Oh yeah, I thought, a fat chance of that.

But to my surprise he came back five minutes later carrying two very thick strong armbands. "I don't believe it," he laughed, "I've just found these on a window sill as though they were waiting for me to pick them up. They look like they'll do the job."

"Great," I said enthusiastically, "let's give them a try."

After fitting the bands around the trainers and the wooly socks I stood up and it worked a treat.

"What do you think Juanito?"

"Superb!" I gloated. "They're really cushioning my feet. The only trouble is the socks will probably wear out after a couple of miles."

Still, we decided to give it a try and set off on our journey. At the outskirts of the village was a little V junction, but sure enough our path was highlighted by a little guiding yellow arrow painted on a stone. Like before, I took longer strides to try and keep pressure off the soles of my feet. The new-fangled idea seemed to be working a treat but once again nature took over. Just nine kilometers to go and I couldn't bear the pain any longer and I sat by the side of the road.

Fred could see the state I was in and made a suggestion. "Juanito, I don't like the idea of leaving you, but I think it's best that I plod on to the albergue to get some help for you."

I could see Fred's concern and I had to agree with him, "Yeah righto mi amigo, I think that's a good idea."

But then, barely minutes after Fred's departure, something else very special happened. I was sat there nursing my wounds when four young Spaniards came marching along well equipped with walking gear.

"Que pasa senor?" asked one in a happy tone.

"Me duelen mucho a las pies mi amigo."

"Ah-h, te sufren a las ampollas."

The young man had enquired how I was and realised I had blisters. He then offered me a drink from a Bota. It was a pouch with a funnel made from pigskin, and it was filled with wine.

"Drink like this," he smiled placing the funnel near his mouth and squirting wine into his mouth.

"Oh great!" I replied eagerly. "That's very kind of you." The red wine soothed the back of my throat and went down like nectar.

To my surprise another young lad stepped forward and thrust a walking staff into my hand.

"Aqui tiene senor, un palo para ayudarte." (Here sir is a stick to help you).

A second lad handed me another staff and repeated the same.

"To help me?" I asked in Spanish.

"Si senor, ven con nosotros por el Camino!" (Yes sir, come and join us on the Camino!).

When I stood up the kind lads even demonstrated how to walk using two poles. Well that was it, I joined these kind pilgrims and walked along with them chatting away in Spanish. The two sticks definitely took pressure off my feet. And besides, I became so engrossed with these young men that my pain seemed to vanish. Along the Way I passed Matthew who was looking worn out. I was now walking so briskly that I actually caught up with Fred. We had just about two miles to go when a land rover came out to meet us. Polly was sat in the passenger seat and she was surprised to see me. She'd actually got in touch with the driver and persuaded him that I needed help. I refused the lift because by now I was thoroughly enjoying the company of these young Spaniards and wanted to finish the route with them. She was so impressed with these young happy men that she decided to join Fred and me and walk along with us. Fred was happy with the situation as it also gave him an opportunity to converse with the Spanish youths. When we reached the albergue the four youngsters informed me that they wanted to carry on to the next village. Keeping in the Spanish mode I thanked them for their help and handed them back their walking staffs.

They took one but then said, "No senor, es un regalo para ti!"

I was greatly touched as he'd actually said that the staff was a present for me. Without any further ado, the young men politely took their leave and departed from the scene. I was certainly touched; I now had a walking staff and a hat, presents given to me by friends on the Camino.

"I can't believe what I've just witnessed," said Polly, "those young men were so beautiful." And then she added with sincere simplicity, "Do you know something John and Fred, I think they were four angels."

"Ha ha!" I laughed, "you could be right there Polly; they certainly seemed to appear from nowhere just to help me in need, and now they've vanished like shadows into the abyss."

It had been an unusual day but all was not yet finished. When I came to take my shoes off there was not a blemish in the woolly socks. I'd just walked almost twelve miles over stony gritty territory and the socks were still in the same condition as when I'd set off.

"It's unbelievable," said Fred as he scrutinised them, "I thought they would have been ripped to shreds; but I can't even find one little hole."

"Yeah Federico and another unbelievable thing is that when I was walking with the four youths it felt as though I was being carried along on a cloud. And now my pain has returned," I laughed as I hobbled into the hostel.

The night was similar to the others but it was tinged with a little sadness as we knew it would be the parting of the ways. We had a last farewell sing-along and then made our way to our beds. Fred nudged me and grinned as Elsina was once again tucked up all nice and snug in the bed next to mine.

Next morning Fred and I bade our farewells to our fellow pilgrims. "Buen Camino and Vaya con Dios!" said Fred to send them on their way. This was an expression that we'd now heard many times along the route and it became second nature for pilgrims to greet each other this way. Just prior to setting off Polly and Elsina each gave Fred and me a small present. They were small cap badges to pin into our hats; I now had three and they were just a few of many yet to come.

It had been a hard yet wonderful experience for Fred and me, but now it was time to make our way back to Barcelona. It had been a harassing experience but the spiritual aspect of it made Fred and I more determined than ever to walk the length of the entire Camino.

"But next time," laughed Fred, "we'll have to be a lot more prepared.

Photos

Mural of a pilgrim on albergue

Relaxing in a bar

Long road ahead

Field of poppies

Fred (My Camino Amigo) with Kristina and Joe Walk

Fred and John Cowell

Santo Domingo pilgrim's meal

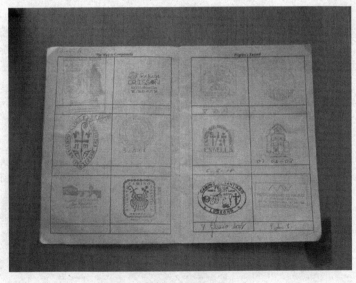

Official albergue passport

Our Blessed Lady in the Wilderness

Ancient gateway in San Jean Pie de Port in France at the start of the Camino

Enjoying a cup of coffee

Monastery on outskirts of Pamplona

Yellow marker pointing the way

Gateway to Camino

The hills of Pamplona

Rest before a steady climb

A mountaintop view

Threatening sky

Happy pilgrims

'Federico'

Onwards and Upwards

Kristina trudging the hills above Pamplona

Still in the hills

The mountains of Ponferado

Haven for birds

Relaxing on humpback bridge

Typical mountain vista

'Federico and Juanito'

Fred, Jenny, Ian and John

Ian, Ronnie, John & Peter at the Ocebriero albergue

Fred below our Blessed Lady's statue

Enchanting dawn in Ocebriero

Another tedious climb (note the yellow arrow)

Fred admiring another statue of Our Blessed Lady

Barry silhouetted at dawn

The 'humble, bumble bee'

De Lorca Albergue

A complimentary swig of wine

Not all days in Spain are sunny

Large rock with yellow arrow

Admiring the poppies

Our Blessed Lady

Barry with his brother John

Venturing into a mountain forest

Paying homage to a memorial

Taking a break

Remember In Your Prayers

Myra Brennan (52 yrs) nee Holland
of Kilkenny and Sligo, Ireland,
who died peacefully in her sleep
in Santiago de Compstella on 24/08/03
having just completed her 2nd consecutive Camino.

And I shall have some peace there

Memorial to John Holland's sister (outskirts of Santiago)

Resting

A cattle drive

Waiting for the albergue in Ocebriero to open

Barry, exhausted and asleep

Pat, Ann and Helen

End of the Way – tired but happy

Pilgrim's meal

Puenta la Reina

Footbathing

Collecting the Compostela Certificate

Statue of Saint James

The last albergue in Compostela

Farewell meal

My Camino Amigo with Helen, Maria and Pat

Chapter Five

The Street Children of Brazil

I had only been home a few days when Fred got in touch with me and he was truly excited. At the time there had been a programme on television about the street children of Brazil, and how cruelly treated they were.

"Look John," he enthused with a godly expression on his face, "we've just got to do something to try and help these pathetic children. The poor wretched creatures have been deserted by their parents and left to their own devices. Many of them are living in sewers beneath the city like rats and are scavenging morsels of food from the gutter. They are living like pack animals and youngsters only ten years old are taking leadership and caring for younger ones."

"Yeah I know what you mean Fred, I've been watching the same programme myself; it's terrible. It seems unbelievable that parents, no matter how poor, would desert their children like that to fend for themselves."

"Look John, I know it's a pathetic state of affairs but I can't condemn the poor people because there but for the grace of God go I. But what I do condemn is the way the barbaric government treat them."

He was right too as the powers that be in Brazil not only refuse to help the poor distraught children in need, the evil government condemn them. So much so that every now and again they organise purges against the so-called *Scourge of the City*. The poor wretched children are then rounded up like vermin by police and executed by a murderous firing squad. A minority of children somehow miraculously manage to survive and hide in the suburbs.

"So what have you got in mind Fred?" I asked knowing only too well that as fellow human beings we needed to do something.

"Well we're going to walk the Camino again John; so I was thinking of putting it to good use."

"Oh yeah, and what have you got in mind?"

"Well I've mentioned the project to CAFOD and that we'd like to walk the Camino to raise money in order to help Brazil's street children. They thought it was a good idea and sent me a load of sponsor forms."

"Right Fred, that means we'll have to get in some serious training."

"Yeah and not only that; well have to try and get as many sponsors as we can."

This was easier said than done. Fred got a lot of sponsors from his church and different work places; he also went onto Radio Lancashire and put a write up in various newspapers. I went around to banks, estate agents, friends and family. Between us both we fared way beyond our expectations. We had hoped to raise a thousand pounds between us but by the time we'd finished we'd raised nearly four thousand pounds for the needy cause.

By now we felt truly committed. As on our trial run of the Camino we trained hard and walked many miles over open moorland to get ourselves into prime condition.

And finally, after weeks of arduous training, our mission day arrived. On our previous walk we had barely walked fifty miles. On this occasion our plan was to walk from Los Arcos to Leon, a distance of nearly two hundred miles.

We flew from Liverpool to Madrid and from there we caught a bus to Los Arcos. It seemed strange to be back in the same albergue from where we had last time waved off our Camino friends. We were up very early next morning and after a sparse breakfast we were ready to set off on our travels. With staff in hand given to me by the four Spanish youths and wearing my gifted hat we hit the road. We were far better equipped this time and we made steady progress without any undue problems. As we walked along through forests and over mountain tracks we sang a song that we had made up about the poor street children. Pilgrims asked us about the song and odd ones contributed towards our cause.

"Buen Camino and Vaya con Dios!" rang in my ears as we passed many pilgrims. Sometimes we stopped at small inns for a coffee and to restock our water supply. This was a good time to chat with fellow travellers and many trinkets were exchanged. Fred and I had brought crucifixes to give out to pilgrims and in return we received more cap badges.

Along the Way we again made many new friends. But one of them stuck out in our minds more than any other. It was a hot day and we came across him as he was refilling his water bottle from a natural fountain. I remember him well because he filled his hat with water and then placed it onto his head. I had to laugh at his funny antics.

"You can laugh all you want sir," he laughed back, "but there's no better way of keeping cool in this heat."

He was right too. I took my hat off and did the same and the cool water rejuvenated my whole body as it spilled down over my face and neck. From then on I filled my hat with cold refreshing water at every opportunity. He was a tall well-built Irish man in his early forties called John Holland. From the very start he was very friendly and enjoyed walking along with us exchanging stories. He tended to walk more with Fred than me as I was a slower walker and tended to lag behind a little.

John had started his pilgrimage in San Juan Pie de Port in France, so he'd already covered 150 kilometers before reaching Los Arcos. Like a lot of other pilgrims he carried a diary with him to record daily events along the route. But unlike others he also had another diary that he read every day. Neither Fred nor I thought anything about it at first, but then we noticed something strange. It happened at the end of a long tiring day's walk.

"How about booking into this albergue," suggested Fred, "it looks quite a good one?"

"Oh I'm sorry, I can't do that," he replied apologetically, "but I need to go a little further." We didn't think anything about it as we thought he might just want to walk a few more kilometers.

Four days into our journey Fred broached the question with John, "How come you always want to stay in certain albergues, have you walked the Camino before?"

"No I haven't, but my elder sister has." It wasn't so much what he said as the way he said it. It was then that he told us a rather poignant story.

"My sister was ten years older than me and she's wanted to walk the Camino for as long as I can remember. Well she did do it and not just once. She actually completed the entire Camino from San Juan Pie de Port to Santiago on two occasions. On her second attempt, last year, she did it with a friend. Along the Way she kept a diary of her everyday events and this is the very one that I am holding in my hands right now."

"Oh yeah," said Fred curiously, "we've noticed you reading that."

John paused for a minute, "Well what it is, she wrote down many details of her journey including every single albergue she stayed in on her way to Santiago."

"Oh she made it to Santiago?" I asked.

I regretted asking that question because his answer knocked me off my feet.

"Oh yes my friend she made it to Santiago alright, but that is as far as she got. You see she actually died that night in her sleep within the albergue."

Well you could have knocked Fred and me down with a feather.

"Oh I'm sorry about that John," said Fred sincerely.

"No need to be sorry," he replied with a smile, "you see my sister was a very religious lady and I think she would have liked it this way. Can you think of a better way of leaving this world?"

"No, I don't think I can, but it's sad all the same."

"I agree with you there Fred and that's the very reason why I want to complete the Journey. I want to walk in my sister's footsteps all the way to Santiago and experience every little hardship that she went through."

After John's moving tale we plodded on and arrived at Santa Domingo de la Calzada. I'd read a lot about different legends in Spain and this town had a very special one. In the middle of the square in front of the mausoleum there is a stone gothic henhouse which was built in the fifteenth century to house a hen and a rooster in memory of the most famous miracle in Santa Domingo de la Calzada.

Documents authenticated by Pope Clements V1 dated 1350 allow live poultry within the cathedral.

Below the cage is a painting by Alphonso Gallego, representing a young boy being hung. Above the cage is a piece of wood from the gallows.

According to legend a young German pilgrim called Hugonell was walking to Santiago de Compostela with his parents and they stayed the night in an inn. The proprietor's daughter immediately fell in love with Hugonell but her love was not reciprocated. She became so angry that she planted a silver cup in his rucksack and then accused him of theft.

Hugonell was found guilty and sentenced to death by hanging. His parents were devastated by his death but still continued their pilgrimage to Santiago. On their return journey they paid a visit to their son's grave. Surprisingly they found that he was still hanging from the gallows, but as they approached him he appeared to move.

"Madre y Padre," he whispered in a weakened voice, "Santa Domingo appeared to me in a dream and has restored me back to life." Quickly the parents rushed to the Mayor's home and informed him of the miracle and asked that their boy be cut down.

The incredulous Mayor who was preparing a feast for friends laughed and responded, "That boy is as alive as these two roast chickens we are about to eat!"

Suddenly to everyone's astonishment the chickens came to life; they sprouted feathers and beaks and began to crow loudly.

The Mayor was left with no alternative but to cut the boy down and grant him his freedom.

"Well that's another legend to add to our archives," said Fred as we made our way back to our albergue.

Next morning we were awaked by the rooster crowing loudly at the crack of dawn. Our next walk took us to San Juan de Ortega, a distance of twenty-eight kilometers. The walk involved climbing a narrow stony gorge which seemed to go upwards forever. Finally we found ourselves on a mountain ridge surrounded on both sides by thick forest. The remaining part of our walk was a gradual descent along a cone-laden path to the sound of many birds. I loved the walk but Fred wasn't taken with it because the forest canopy kept us constantly in the shade. After a few hours we took a break and sustained ourselves with jam, crispy bread and water. During our respite lots of walkers passed us and none of them were carrying rucksacks.

"Hey how come they don't have any rucksacks Juanito?"

"I'm not sure Federico; maybe they're locals just out for a stroll."

"U-um, I don't think so somehow; I think I'll ask them."

"Oh no we're not locals," was the reply, "we're pilgrims on the Camino."

"But where are your rucksacks?" asked Fred. "How can you possibly make it without provisions?"

Well the answer took Fred and me completely by surprise. "Oh when we reach the next village there'll be a coach waiting to take us back to our hotel."

"Hotel!" gasped Fred. "Do you mean to say you won't be stopping in an albergue?"

"No way," was the reply, "we're all booked into a hotel for a week."

"And how does that work?"

"Well tomorrow morning after breakfast the coach will bring us back to where we finish our walk today."

"So you mean to say the coach drops you off and picks you up every day at different spots?"

"That's right my friend," he replied calmly, "can you think of a better way of walking the Camino?"

Fred just smiled as he was stuck for words. "Well that's it," he said as we carried on walking again, "I've heard it all now; that's a cushy way to do a pilgrimage." I agreed with Fred that it didn't seem in keeping with the spirit of the Camino.

We finally arrived in San Juan de Ortega late afternoon and sure enough there was a coach waiting to pick up the light-footed travellers. Fred and I were tired but the irony of it was that we couldn't refresh ourselves as all facilities were taken up by the bus riders.

It was a hot day and I was tired and dehydrated and badly needed to cool down. "Blow this for a tale Fred I'm going to have a wash down in that horse trough over there." I did as well. I not only had a wash; I stripped down to my shorts and sprawled out in the cold refreshing water. It may sound a crazy thing to do but I thoroughly enjoyed that soaking. It took my mind back to when I used to do silly things as a lad. Later on we met up with John Holland again inside the albergue. It was run by monks and they specialised in making various menus. As we had dinner Fred volunteered to wait upon the tables and he dished out bowls of delicious soup.

The following day we walked with this special Irish gentleman until we reached the city of Burgos. It had been raining hard during the night and the dusty mountain tracks were thick with sludge. As we trudged along in knee-deep thick mud my feet went from underneath me and I landed flat on my back. Luckily my rucksack cushioned my fall. But as I tried to stand up it was like watching a comedy act as I slid all over the place. By the time I'd struggled back onto my feet I was like a clay man out of a Flash Gordon movie.

As we entered the city a festival was taking place and we could hear singing and loud music. After enjoying a colourful spectacle we attended a celebratory mass in Burgos Cathedral. I felt rather conspicuous as we walked down the aisle to receive Holy Communion in my clay suit. However, none of the congregation seemed to mind.

It was after the ceremony that the gallant Irishman informed us that he'd arranged to meet up with his family who were flying in from Ireland.

"I'm sorry gentlemen," he said sincerely, "but this is the parting of the ways as I will be staying here in Burgos for a few days before making my way to Santiago." After briskly shaking hands he bade us farewell with the very familiar words, "Buen Camino!"

"Y tu mismo mi amigo," said Fred. (And the same to you my friend.)

We never set eyes on John again. But sometime way in the future, along the Camino, we were to come across something very touching about him and his sister.

The next stretch of territory after Burgos opened up into thousands of square kilometers of flat open wilderness known as the

Meseta. Unlike walking along mountain paths there was hardly any shade.

"Blooming' 'eck Federico, it's flaming' hot on this Meseta," I grunted as the sun got higher in the sky, "I think I'd rather be back up in the mountains."

"Aye it is and it beats me why they call it the Meseta as it stretches out for miles in front of us."

I had to laugh because Fred was referring to the fact that Meseta translates to *Little Table*.

Luckily we'd been forewarned to make sure we'd enough water as fountains were few and far between in this parched area. Crossing the vast Meseta we passed through a patchwork landscape of orchards, vineyards and pastures of red poppies. It was a sight to behold as the flowers swayed gently in a breeze and the red colour blended superbly with green patches of grass.

We only walked twenty-five kilometers that day and gradually arrived at a tiny hamlet. There was no inn to have a pilgrim's meal but along with other pilgrims we conjured up something. It was a kind of *Jacob's Join* where we each contributed a little food towards a meal. It was very basic but the community spirit more than made up for it. An elderly man sat at the head of a table and said grace before meals. After the sparse meal we said a few prayers for our fellow pilgrims. As we retired to our bunks the elder handed us some papers written in Spanish. One was an inscription of the LORD'S PRAYER and the other was the HAIL MARY.

Once again we had to sleep in an old barn. "Oh here we go again," said Fred, "I only hope it's not as cold as the one in Estella."

But we needn't have worried; on this occasion we both had sleeping bags with us and slept well.

On the trail next day, Fred and I conversed in Spanish and learned our two new sets of prayers. We both enjoyed the challenge and before we knew it we were approaching our next albergue. It was here that something rather funny happened. The hostel was only small with eight beds crammed together. In the next two beds close to me was an elderly Italian couple and they were not very talkative.

"Perhaps it's because they don't speak English," said Fred.

"Yeah, maybe you're right Federico," I replied zipping up my sleeping bag.

But then at three o'clock in the morning I woke up bursting to go to the loo. I was a bit dreary-eyed and I couldn't find my torch. No matter, I tried fumbling around in pitch darkness to make my way to the toilet. As I tried walking I stood on a boot and fell head over heels onto the Italian lady's bed. She was obviously startled and the commotion woke up everybody in the room.

Oh 'eck, I thought, I'm in for it now! I expected a right grilling from the Italian guy but that couldn't have been further from the truth. Both he and his wife were both overly concerned for my wellbeing.

In pigeon English they both expressed their concern asking if I was alright. "You no hurt yourself sir?" he asked shining his torch. "I keep light for you to go toilet sir." I picked myself up feeling rather embarrassed thanking them for their concern.

Next morning the kind couple approached me again to make sure I was alright.

"Eh Juanito, I'll tell you what," laughed Fred as we strolled along, "that was nice of that Italian guy last night wasn't it; especially after you dived onto his wife?"

"It was that Federico, and to think we thought they were a miserable pair."

"Ha ha! the Camino never fails to impress me."

Trudging along we finally came to the end of the Meseta. From there on in we started climbing again and from the highland we looked back on mile upon mile of fertile valleys.

The days passed by and the friendliness and spiritual feeling along the Way continued. Fred and I carried first aid kits in our rucksacks and they came in handy on various occasions as pilgrims suffered from blisters and other painful ailments.

On our penultimate day we finished up in a *Way Out West* type of town and our lodging was in a hayloft.

It was in this village that we met three American girls and all three were suffering from blisters. After putting my nursing expertise to good use the young ladies had lunch with us in a small inn. I can't recall their names but all three came across as plucky and adventurous. After a pleasant evening we made our way back to the hayloft. Surprisingly it turned out to be the best night's sleep I'd had in a while.

On our last day's walk to Leon, we walked along with the courageous ladies. We stopped a few times along the way as their blisters were playing up and creating a lot of pain. I knew how they felt having suffered a similar experience. Be that as it may, the plucky ladies struggled on and finally made it to the city. That afternoon we had a few wines and a pilgrim's meal with them prior to wishing them, "Buen Camino!"

But for Fred and me our Camino had come to an end. We had fulfilled our promise and finished our task of aiding the poor wretched street children of Brazil.

But Fred was keener now than ever to continue in his good works.

"Jaunito," he said as we made our way back to Madrid Airport, "this pilgrimage is one of many; we must come back again to complete the walk from here to Santiago."

I just smiled at him. How could I refuse this man.

Chapter Six

Santiago de Compostela

We'd no sooner got back home before Fred was calling upon my services once again. Sometimes it was to visit a school to give one of his lectures or to help out with an organ recital in Salford Cathedral or some other major building. He worked extremely hard for his local church and organised jumble sales or anything else to raise funds. Twice a year he arranged fun days in Heaton Park, Manchester, including walking or running around the grounds. We'd set off early on a Sunday morning and set up tents and stalls for lady volunteers. After setting up we'd then put on CAFOD vests and act as stewards. Our main task was to stand at various junctions in the park and guide runners and walkers to the next point. This could be rather tedious as we could be there for hours on end… especially if it was raining. Still, I've got to admit I always felt better at the end of the day. To give Fred his due, his enthusiasm for doing good works was boundless; and it tended to rub off on me.

"Are you ready for our next Camino John?" he asked as we made our way home.

"Well I suppose I'm as ready as I'll ever be," I replied, "what have you got planned for us this time?"

Just like Liberia his next good cause was to set up schools and build water wells in one of Africa's impoverished countries.

Consequently, weeks passed by and once again we were heading for Spain. We started our Camino where we had finished our last one in Leon. We'd no sooner set off along the Way before we heard the regular refrain of "Buen Camino!"

"Oh we're back," laughed Fred, "let's go for it Juanito." We were rather tired that day as we hadn't arrived at our albergue till late the previous night and were feeling rather jetlagged. Consequently we only walked fifteen kilometers. It paid off though as it gave us ample time to rest and prepare our gear for next day. Once again we made many friends and some were memorable. One of these was called Ronnie and he was a character. He was definitely oriental but could speak English and lived in Holland.

After introductions he turned to Fred and said, "Nice to meet you Freddy, I'm Ronnie." On turning to me he started laughing and said in a funny tone, "Nice to meet you too; I'm Ronni-i-e-ee, Johnni-i-e-ee!" Fred and I started laughing at his funny mannerisms and from that moment on it carried on in this vein. If he happened to see us on the Camino he'd shout in a hilarious voice, "Johnni-i-e-ee!" And Fred and I would respond by "Ronni-i-e-ee!" Likewise, if I saw him first I would shout, "Ronni-i-e-ee," and he would respond accordingly. It certainly struck a chord with passing pilgrims as they burst out laughing at our funny antics. Ronnie had set a precedent and, for the rest of our walk to Santiago, it became a ritual and created lots of laughter.

After a couple of days we arrived in Astorga, a famous historical town. Fred and I had frequented many churches on our travels but we especially wanted to visit a particular one in this town.

As we approached the magnificent building we were certainly impressed by its structure and outstanding architecture. But on entering the church we were both appalled and somewhat disappointed by what we saw. The walls, ceiling, altar and even the floor were completely adorned in gold. It actually made us feel sick as there must have been millions of pounds decorating the entire place.

"Oh I don't believe this," said Fred, "to me this is showing off. All this money going to waste when there are so many needy causes throughout the world. It may well be the most famous church in Spain but to me it's not a house of God."

"That's my sentiments entirely Federico," I reiterated, "you've just taken the words right out of my mouth. Come on, let's get out of here." Along the Camino we'd frequented many churches and always said a prayer; sadly we didn't say one in this wealthy church.

The next place we came across was Rabanal, a quaint little hamlet and we had a break at a little café. And this is where we met an Australian couple, or so we thought. The man, called Ian, was definitely Australian from Sydney but his lady friend, Jenny, was from South Africa. We hit it off with the couple straightaway and they had a coffee with us.

"Do you know that the building next door is a monastery," said Ian, "and it's famous for its singing monks?"

"Oh I've heard about it," replied Fred, "I believe that pilgrims can stay there for the night."

"That's right," said Jenny who'd been reading about it in a guide book, "and the monks wait on you during the evening meal."

"U-um, I wouldn't mind staying here for the night Juanito," said Fred, "how about you?"

"Yeah I'm up for that Federico, it sounds Interesting. How about you two Ian and Jenny?"

"No not really, it may sound interesting but there's one snag."

"And what's that Ian?" asked Fred.

He just smiled, "Well all the monks are sworn to a vow of silence. And any pilgrim who stays there is committed to the same vow. So now do you still fancy staying there?"

"Sworn to silence," I asked, "what about the singing?"

111

"Oh that's only at certain ceremonies, but after that they stick devoutly to their vow."

"Ha ha," laughed Fred, "I'm still gam' if John is. Anyway what about you two?"

Ian just gave a cheeky grin and winked, "Well I'd be alright, but there's no way that Jenny could keep silent for so long … you know what women are like."

"Hey, don't be so cheeky I ….."

"It's alright Jenny … I was only kidding."

"Yes and you'd better be," she smiled giving him a gentle tap around his head.

"No lads, all joking aside, we won't be stopping here because we have a really tight schedule. We've decided to go on to the next village which is another nine kilometers from here and it's a long treacherous uphill climb over wild open territory. Anyway gentlemen, we're going to have to get going because, by the looks of those dark clouds, it looks as though we're in for a storm."

"Yeah righto," replied Fred, "maybe we'll see you both later along the Way."

"Yeah maybe you will; we hope so. Anyway my friends ... Buen Camino!"

In hindsight we should have gone with them because ten minutes later we discovered that the monastery was full.

"Well that doesn't leave us with any option," laughed Fred. "Vamos Juanito, we'd better get our skates on too!"

Making our way up a gritty mountain road, we'd about three kilometers to go when the heavens opened. We had some wet gear with us but by the time we reached the village we were drenched to the skin. Gale force winds swept icy rain into our faces. The temperature dropped dramatically and both of us were frozen to the bone. To our disappointment this albergue was also full. It turned out that Ian and Jenny had got the last two beds. We were offered a stable but windows were broken and a large barn door didn't shut properly. To make matters worse there were no beds; just mattresses on a stone cobbled floor.

113

"Blimey," said Fred, "it's freezing in here and it's still daytime. We can't stay here Juanito, it's even colder than the one in Estella."

"Too true we can't," I mumbled through quivering lips, "we'd freeze to death before morning. Anyway, the first thing we've got to do is to get out of these wet clothes as quick as we can."

Luckily there was a private hostel not too far from the albergue. It cost us thirty-five Euros each but we had little option. It was a case of either pay up or freeze to death.

"Hey this is great Juanito," said Fred as we entered our room, "there's a hot shower; this is like home from home." The room was only basic but after what we'd experienced it was luxury. After a warm shower we felt great and made our way to a little inn to have a pilgrim's meal with our fellow travellers. A good night was enjoyed by all as we chatted away and then had a sing along. During the meal we conversed a lot with Ian and Jenny and they were to become our travelling companions for the next few days. Along the Way something very funny happened. Ian and Jenny were rather affectionate with each other and after a long day's trek they liked nothing more than having a cuddle in one of their beds. Well it turned out that one particular evening we got digs together in a monastery. After resting up, Ian and Jenny decided to go in search of a shower. So with towels in hand they walked along a corridor and climbed some stairs. To their amazement they came across a bathroom.

"Wow, this is a nice surprise," said Jenny, "this is a first along the Camino."

"You're not kidding," replied Ian with a big smile on his face, "how about giving our poor aching bones a good soaking?"

"What, together?"

"Yeah, why not, have you got any better ideas; we've never had the opportunity before?"

Well the temptation was too much; so it was off with their clothes and into the bathtub. They were thoroughly enjoying themselves when there was a knock on the door. They didn't answer and the knocking persisted. As the knocks turned into raps, Ian and Jenny struggled to suppress the giggles. Gradually the knocking finished and they both discreetly made their way back into the albergue. Everything seemed to go un-noticed until we were having our evening meal along with some monks. After the meal one of the monks stood up and gave the usual blessing. It was then that he mentioned that the local priest wasn't too happy as someone had been using his private bathroom.

"Oh 'eck!" blushed Jenny, "I hope he doesn't find out there were two of us in his royal suite; that would put him in a happy mood."

It was then that we realised what had happened and we all cracked out laughing. Even the monks had to smile. Consequently, next morning Ian and Jenny made a hasty exit before breakfast to avoid the priest's wrath. Their little escapade created a happy atmosphere amongst the pilgrims and spurred everybody onwards even when the spirit was flagging.

Every now and again we came across more memorials of bygone pilgrims. One that sticks in mind was of a Japanese man who had travelled from the other side of the world. A translation read, *Plucked from the Camino and taken from this world to the next.*

"Aye that's a nice inscription Juanito," said Fred, "God must have picked him up in his arms and carried him off to Heaven."

"Yeah Federico, along with all the other poor souls we've come across along the Way."

Gradually we came across a little village approaching Ponferado. The albergue was full but we were offered tents to sleep in.

I wasn't feeling too well and just needed to rest. "That'll do me Federico, because I don't think I could walk another step."

As soon as we booked in I went straight to the tent. It was only afternoon but I was completely jaded. I had a word with Fred. "If you don't mind Federico I don't feel like going out for a meal, I just need to rest." The strange thing is I slept like a baby in that tent right through until next morning and I woke up completely invigorated.

Along with other pilgrims we approached Ponferada and as we passed a little café we heard the familiar sound of Johni-i-e-ee! After an automatic response we joined him for a coffee.

Back on the Camino the route climbed steadily higher and higher. Traipsing tediously over gritty winding paths we gradually arrived at Cacabellos, a small village surrounded by high mountains. On the outskirts of the small village we passed underneath a motorway that had been recently been built across a mountain range. It was a magnificent feat of engineering and had been built from European funds at a cost of millions of pounds. Large concrete pillars about eighty meters high supported the great highway. We could see large wagons driving way above us and they looked like dinky toys.

"Wow, just look at that autopista Federico!" I said as I gazed upwards in amazement at the gigantic structure, "it must have cost a bomb to build that."

"You're not kidding Juanito, and to think that thirty years ago Spanish roads were just like dirt tracks."

Our thoughts on the structure were interrupted as we heard a voice calling from behind us, "Johni-i-e-ee!"

On turning, both Fred and I shouted back in unison "Roni-i-e-ee!"

Passing pilgrims laughed and started singing, Ronni-e-ee and Johnni-e-ee." It was just one of those catchy things that trigger off people's imagination. Everybody admitted that it certainly took their minds off their feet.

In the next village we stayed at an albergue run by Brazilians. It turned out to be a pleasant stay as we listened to their type of music.

The following day was only twenty kilometers but it was a steep uphill climb all the way. We headed for a mountaintop village called O'Cebriero and the views were spectacular. The trek was hard going but we were rewarded with beautiful rolling countryside, wild flowers and rocky ox cart tracks and lush mountains formed an unbelievable backdrop. By the time we arrived at the mountain abode we were way above the clouds. Above us was an azure clear sky just like being in an airplane. Tiny villages and green farmlands could be made out as we looked downwards through dispersing clouds. It was much cooler in the mountain village and views all around were breathtaking. To describe the vistas and the atmosphere of this awesome place is just too hard to put into writing.

When we arrived at the albergue there were many rucksacks stacked in lines as pilgrims waited around for the hostel to open. Ian and Jenny gave us a hearty greeting. Many of the pilgrims were feeling tired, dehydrated and a little downcast but that all changed when a certain pilgrim arrived.

"Johni-i-e-ee!" rang out a voice from the edge of the village.

Fred and I automatically responded in a long melodious tone, "Ronni-i-e-ee!"

It was really funny as everyone, as though synchronized by a spiritual conductor, started singing in unison, "Ronni-i-e-ee .... Johni-i-e-ee!"

"Eh-h, come here Ronnie and have a drink with us!" said Fred as he opened a bottle of wine.

That night in the albergue above the clouds a group of pilgrims from Brazil, Italy, Germany, Australia, America, Canada and many other countries gathered together and sang along with each other in perfect harmony. It was a joy to behold.

During the evening we got talking to an Australian gentleman called Peter who was walking the Camino with his wife and daughter. They had already trekked from San Juan Pie de Port in France, a distance of nearly seven hundred kilometers. During our conversation he told us a rather poignant yet happy tale. Their daughter was in her early thirties and during her teenage years had got into bad company and become involved in drugs and really gone off the rails. She had lived in her parents' home but had given them so much hassle that they couldn't cope anymore. Consequently, despite loving her, they threatened to throw her out onto the street unless she changed her ways. She behaved for a while but gradually drifted back into the drug scene.

"It's amazing," said Peter, "how she lied, cheated and deceived us. She was so convincing that my wife and I truly believed she'd kicked the habit. But it came to light when I actually caught her using a needle in her bedroom. Lo and behold she started screaming and throwing things at me. She smashed ornaments and started raving like a mad person. My wife and I were at our wits end and we had no alternative but to call the police and have her removed from our home."

"Oh I'm sorry." said Fred sincerely, "that's really sad."

"Yes it was," replied Peter with a glint in his eye, "but then a kind of miracle happened. My wife and I were devastated, but then I happened to bump into an old friend who'd just been on the Camino. I can't explain it but a strange feeling of hope overcame me. After discussing it with my wife we asked our daughter if she would do the entire route with us from France to Santiago. We agreed that if she completed the task we would let her return home. She was rather reluctant, but consented as it appeared to be the lesser of two evils."

"And is this the girl who is with you now?" asked Fred.

"That's right," smiled Peter, "and believe me she's a changed girl. She was rather grumpy all the way on our flight from Australia and even more so as we made our way by train to San Juan Pie de Port."

"So what happened?" I enquired becoming intrigued with his tale. "She appears to be a very happy young lady to me."

"Well that's it," he blurted excitedly, "you see, she has now become our kind considerate little girl again. And the miraculous change seemed to start more or less on our first day's walk. The friendliness of all the pilgrims and the spiritual atmosphere had a definite affect on her. Instead of selfishly thinking of herself all the time she began to help elderly pilgrims who were struggling. It was as though she had a magical cloak wrapped about her and she was changing in front of our very eyes. Every foot of the way from then on she's gone from strength to strength." He paused for a minute and looked his daughter's way and came out with something very touching. "And just look at her now; it's as though God has given our little girl back to us!"

Fred and I just looked at each other and smiled.

When we retired to our beds there was a stillness about the place. As I lay in bed recounting the beautiful evening Fred nudged me, "I'll tell you what Juanito, there was definitely a magical atmosphere in that room tonight; I'll remember it for the rest of my life."

He was right too because I felt the same: it was one of those once in a lifetime moments … a memory that will last forever.

Needless to say we were both soon in 'Noddy land' only to be woken by an early morning call.

As we left the village the view was completely different. We couldn't see any villages below us or any of the surrounding hills as thick white billowing clouds floated in the heavens beneath us. The first lap of our journey was downhill and as we walked through the clouds it gave us a feeling as though we were floating on air. It was rather chilly but after covering a few miles we were revelling in bright sunshine and serene hills.

After taking photos of the unusual scenery we once again made tracks to our next port of call. Many good-feeling events continued to crop up as we passed through various mountain villages. But one thing that amused Fred and me was that little old ladies would run up to us and offer us bread and supply us with fresh water. In one small hamlet a little old lady approached us and actually gave us pancakes.

The next major town we came across was Portomarin.

"There must be a main port in this town Juanito by the sound of its name."

Fred was right too. In fact, to access the town we had to cross over a large bridge which spanned a magnificent river. It was in this small town that we met Monika, a Spanish lady, who happened to be a doctor.

She was intrigued with Fred and me as she'd never come across an English person before who could speak Spanish. Every now and again along the Way we'd bump into her and she'd walk along with us for a few miles. It was on this stretch of our journey that we came across a little old Chinese lady carrying a black plastic bag. She was only slight and rather bent over and didn't appear to talk English or Spanish. But that didn't deter her at all. As she plodded on at a snail's pace she kept bending down to pick up rubbish that had been strewn along the Way. The little lady shamed all three of us into picking up odd cartons and other bits of litter as we strolled along. She was only a slow walker but for the next three days we kept bumping into her. She may not have realised it, but she became a talking point amongst the pilgrims. Her simple way of life rendered everyone who met her into a humble state.

Fred was a better walker than me but one day, as we walked through a tiny hamlet, he stopped me in my tracks. "Juanito, how about stopping here for the night?"

"How come Federico," I responded, "it's only eleven o'clock and we've only covered ten kilometers?"

"Aye I know that, but how about having a lazy day to give us a break?"

"Yeah righto mi amigo if that's what you want." So that was it. We booked into a tiny albergue and settled down for the day.

"Oh this is great," said Fred as he sprawled out sunbathing on a grassy patch of land.

The rest did us both good and refreshed our energy and determination.

Along the Way we bumped into Ian and Jenny again and for the following two nights we stayed in the same albergue and shared an evening meal with them.

The days passed and on our penultimate night we happened to be in the same albergue as Monika. During the evening meal she asked Fred and I what made us do the Camino. Fred being a modest fellow asked me to enlighten her. After I'd finished talking she was very impressed and handed me fifty Euros toward our needy cause. To say the least, Fred and I were rather surprised. And then she came out with something rather touching,

"I'm from the Basque country in Northern Spain and when I'm feeling at a low ebb, I love to walk this stretch of the Camino. I enjoy the company of other pilgrims but on my final day's walk into Santiago I have always done it alone; but it would be a favour if you two gentlemen would allow me to walk with you tomorrow."

"You're more than welcome," answered Fred, "in fact it would be an honour to escort you into the great city."

"Salud y Vaya con Dios!" I said raising a glass of wine, "Estoy de acuerdo con Federico." (Cheers and God bless you ... I agree with Federico).

So we did march into Santiago along with Monika. It was yet another great opportunity to practice our Spanish. The first place we headed for was the cathedral. Luckily we got there just in time for mass. During the service four monks got together and started pulling vigorously on long dangling ropes. Hanging from the highest part of the roof was a large pendulum which started to swing from one side of the cathedral to the other. As the monks continually pulled down on the ropes the huge pendulum swung higher and higher, almost touching the high ceiling. As it built up momentum it cast lots of incense into the air. To watch it in action was a thrilling and dramatic event, as it swung way up to the ceiling and then downward casting fumes of incense onto the congregation my stomach did a flip.

"By 'eck," I stuttered as it floated close above people's heads, "it looks rather dangerous to me."

Monika nudged me and just laughed, "Not to worry Juanito, in nearly a thousand years only two people have been killed." She also enlightened us that the pendulum was called a 'Botafumeiro' and that it was a tradition handed down from way back in the Middle Ages.

"What it is," she said, "is that pilgrims back then didn't have the same hygienic facilities that we have today. By the time they reached Santiago their clothes were in tatters and, to put it mildly, they literally stank like sewer rats. The incense was to try and combat the terrible stench."

After leaving the cathedral we made our way to an albergue and had a shower prior to a pilgrim's meal. During the evening we came across Peter, his wife and daughter; and the young lady looked great. In fact she had a kind of radiance about her. Fred and I had a talk with the girl and her eyes seemed to light up as she talked about her experience on the Camino. Because of the outcome Peter and his wife were obviously ecstatic and they too had a special vibrancy about them.

Once again we were amazed at all the spiritual happenings that kept cropping up during our inspired experience on the Camino. We'd actually finished our pilgrimage with time to spare which gave us ample time to explore the city. Ironically we never bumped into Ian and Jenny whilst in Santiago, but we were destined to meet up with them again in future years.

The day arrived for us to make our way home and we ordered a taxi to take us to Santiago Airport. On the way through busy traffic Fred spotted Ronnie. We wound the window down and started to shout in unison, Ronni-i-e-ee!

Ronnie's ears pricked up and he shouted gleefully from amidst a vast crowd Johni-i-e-ee!...Johni-i-e-ee! We could see him waving and we responded until he faded into the distance. It was a befitting end to a glorious pilgrimage.

On this occasion we didn't raise as much money as our first walk but we still fared very well.

"Well that's it," I thought to myself on reaching home, "I can have a well earned rest now." But I had a sneaky feeling that Fred had something else up his sleeve. I was right too. After reaching Santiago he was hungry for more of the same.

Hence, in the following years we covered every stretch of the Camino de Frances several times in order to raise money for other deserving causes. This included walking from San Jaun Pie de Port in France to Burgos on three separate occasions, a distance of nearly two hundred miles.

Our first day's walk from San Juan involved a steep nineteen kilometer climb to the peak of the Pyrenees Mountains. Half way up the mountain we met up with Pedro and Maria, a friendly Spanish couple and they were engrossed with a statue of Our Blessed Lady standing alone on top of a stony ridge overlooking inaccessible wilderness and beauty. All four of us were overawed by the spiritual site and felt the need to say a prayer. From that moment on we became special friends. I gave a crucifix to each of them and they gave me a badge for my hat to go with many others.

Three hours later we reached the peak which gave way to fertile valleys and pine forests of Spain. As I looked downwards I sighed with relief as I thought I had done the hardest part of the day's walk. But I had a rude awaking as the nine kilometer descent into Roncesvalles played havoc on my knees. Hours later we arrived in Roncesvalles, a historical town. That evening we enjoyed a pilgrim's meal with our new-found friends. In fact we walked with them for the next three days stopping over in Zubiri, Pamplona and finally Puente la Reina. Before parting they gave us a typical Spanish blessing. Pedro gave us both a bear hug and Maria gave us a kiss on both cheeks.

"Federico y Jaunito, los dos son amigos tan especiales; cuidate y Vaya con Dios!" said Pedro as we parted company. (Fred and John, you are two very special friends; take care and go with God!).

We never expected to set eyes on them again, but God had other plans in mind.

The following morning I was looking forward to seeing a special place: at least it was special to me. We were on our way to Estella.

The sun was high in the sky and I vented my feeling to Fred, "It shouldn't be too long now Federico before we come across that old Roman bridge; I m really looking forward to seeing it again."

Ha ha!" he laughed. "And so you should be; this is where our first little miracle happened. Do you remember me finding those trainers?"

"Too true I can; what a relief that was. Anyway I can't wait to soak my feet in the river again by the side of that old Roman bridge."

We were both eager to set eyes on this special spot again but alas it had totally changed. The ancient bridge had been demolished and been replaced by a much wider modern bridge.

"Oh no I don't believe it," I gasped as I set eyes on the place, "they've gone and knocked down that old Roman bridge."

I felt rather sad as it held special memories for me, and Fred made it plain that he felt the same as I did. "E-eh, what a shame; all in the name of progress. Never mind Juanito; they can't take our memories from us."

We were both rather disappointed with the outcome but, all the same, we decided to rest and soak our feet once again in the welcoming river.

During the next few days we made our way through many mountain hamlets and finally arrived at the city of Burgos.

"This place puts me in mind of John Holland, the Irishman, who was following in his sister's footsteps," said Fred, "this is where we last saw him."

"Yeah me too Federico; I wonder if he made it to Santiago."

We didn't know it then but all would be revealed to us years later on our travels.

Another time when we started our pilgrimage from San Juan, an Englishman called Joe Walk joined us. The thought struck me that it was quite an appropriate name for walking the Camino. Joe was a French teacher and I was quite impressed with him because, after finishing his pilgrimage, he had already arranged to spend two years in Nigeria to help teach some underprivileged children. On this particular Camino, Kristina, a young Hungarian girl, also started the walk with us. She was very taken with Fred and she appeared to have a teenage crush on him. It may well be that she looked upon him as a father figure. Fred being the man he is took her under his wing and constantly gave her advice on how to cope along the Way. During the evening meals she always managed to sit herself by his side. I teased him a little as he had done with me when the Dutch lady, Elsina, seemed to be rather fond of me. Five days into the Camino we had a pleasant experience. The sun was high in the sky and fiercely beating down. We were all feeling its effects when we came across a monastery. It was closed but we had access to a brass wine tap with a notice displayed above it which read "Fill your bottle my pilgrim friends and refresh yourselves for the journey in hand." Other pilgrims had congregated there and the atmosphere was truly heartwarming. It really was a good experience and revived people when their spirits were flagging. It was a special moment to remember but sadly, later that day, we came across the worst albergue that I had ever experienced. It was a private hostel run by Colombians. It became evident that they were far more interested in making money than the plight of their pilgrim friends. Inside the building it was like a rabbit warren and toilet facilities were almost non-existent. There were no beds, just mattresses on a concrete floor; and the greedy owners had crammed as many into each tiny room as possible. To make matters worse it was very cold with no heating. About three o'clock in the morning I hadn't slept a wink. As I made my way in total darkness clambering over bodies I decided I'd had enough. I rumbled through my rucksack and packed my gear ready for the off.

"What's up Juanito?" said Fred shining a light in my eyes.

"What's up?" I replied grumpily, "I'm not staying in this flea-ridden-pit another minute!"

"But it's pitch black outside; how are you going to find your way over the mountain tracks?"

"Don't worry about it Federico, I'll manage somehow; anything's better than staying in this dump!"

Well I did set off and it was rather daunting at first and even a little scary. But two hours later it started to come light and birds began to sing. Things now appeared much brighter and I actually enjoyed walking in the clean morning air. I walked as far as Aviano and had a welcoming breakfast in a village cafe. Fred, Joe and Kristina gradually caught up with me.

Fred and I did a third Camino from San Juan and the friendliness and loyalty amongst the pilgrims continued. I thought I'd seen everything on the Camino but then one morning as we left Roncesvalles we came across two ladies in their thirties. One of them was struggling badly with blisters as she plodded along. The other lady had a fine physique but I couldn't believe what I was witnessing. She had her own rucksack on her back and was actually carrying her mate's rucksack in her arms in front of her. We offered to help but they refused saying that they'd started the pilgrimage together and were determined to get by alone as they thought it unfair to burden other pilgrims. I didn't think they would get very far but they proved me wrong. Six days later in Los Arcos they stayed in the same albergue as Fred and me and actually invited both of us to join them in a meal of spaghetti bolognaise which they'd cooked themselves.

Some time later after completing another Camino, Fred and I made our way to Lourdes in France to help out with the many disabled people who go there on pilgrimage every year. We were both taken aback by the number of wheelchairs; there were literally thousands of them. Whilst in the holy town we were kitted out with special jackets denoting we were assistants. We were also given two flagged badges to wear denoting that we spoke both English and Spanish. We worked there for a week helping out on the railway station, the airport and the baths. Every night after a hard day's work we volunteered to work in the Grotto where Our Blessed Lady appeared to Saint Bernadette over one hundred and fifty years ago. Both Fred and I felt that it was a great honour to have this special duty. It was our job to organise a vast crowd of people eagerly waiting to pass through the Grotto and we both took the task very seriously.

One evening whilst on duty we heard a loud voice coming from the vast crowd. "Federico y Juanito!" It was none other than our special friends Pedrito and his wife Maria, whom we'd walked with two years earlier and Pedrito was wearing the crucifix I'd given him. It turned out to be the first time that they had ever visited Lourdes too. So to come across them amongst thousands of people seemed incredible. It was a special moment for all four of us and they greeted us in a familiar friendly way, "Vaya con Dios!" It seemed so fitting to meet up with them in such a holy place.

Friends on the Camino are truly special and this also proved true of Ian and Jenny, the Australian couple, whom we had met on a previous pilgrimage.

In between pilgrimages, Ian rang Fred to inform us that they were holidaying in Nice, Southern France. "Hi Fred, Ian here; I'm ringing from Nice in France. Jenny and I are staying here in a villa and we'll be here for three months. We've done a temporary house swap and the owners of this house are over in Australia stopping at our house."

"Oh that's handy Ian, maybe you'll be able to pop over to England and see us."

"Ha ha!" laughed Ian. "That's funny because Jenny and I want to know if you two will come over to France and stop here with us for a while."

"It sounds good to me Ian. I'll tell you what, I'll get in touch with John and I'll get back to you."

Well Fred did get in touch with me and I was all for it. Within a week we flew over to Nice and spent ten fantastic days in the French Riviera. They picked us up at the airport and ran us all over the place. One unforgettable place was Monaco's boat harbour with its impressive yachts. I was also intrigued at the height and splendour of the Alps Mountain Range. They were perfect hosts and Jenny put on a splendid meal every night to make us feel at home. At the end of a fabulous break they then escorted us safely back to the airport. A year later they came over to England and stopped at my house for a few days.

Some time later Ian and Jenny walked the Camino again; but this time they started their walk from Seville in Southern Spain. Fred and I met up with them along the way and walked with them as far as Salamanca. By this time Fred and I had become rather well known on the Camino and for some reason we got tagged with the nickname, 'The Two Rascals'.

In between Caminos Fred continued to call upon me to help out with CAFOD events.

Our escapades became so well known that my younger brother, Barry, became interested and he asked me if I would do a Camino with him. Fred was holidaying with his family in Turkey and so I decided to take him on but insisted that I take the lead.

"Oh I promise you our John, I'll do anything that you advise me to do," Barry replied eagerly.

He was so keen that he begged me to walk the entire Camino with him in one go all the way to Santiago. And so after a lot of thought I arranged a flight to Lourdes in France and we took a train to San Juan Pie de Port. To celebrate the occasion we had our first pilgrim's meal in the ancient historical village. Next morning as we strutted upwards and onwards on the gritty slopes of the Pyrenees Mountains, vultures hovered in the blue sky above us.

"Bloomin' 'eck our John," Barry joked as sweat dripped from his brow. "I hope they're not a sign of things to come."

"Not to worry our Barry," I replied, "vultures around these parts were almost extinct a few years ago but the Spanish government have put a recovery plan into effect to help them survive. Carcasses of cattle are scattered around the wilderness below for the vultures to scavenge on."

With that sorted out we struggled on and gradually came across the statue of Our Blessed Lady welcoming us with open arms. Our Barry was overwhelmed by the holy sight and couldn't wait to scramble over jagged rocks to be near her. Overwhelming joy became apparent when he discovered a tiny insect struggling at her feet; the tiny creature happened to be a bumble bee. The reason for his ecstasy was because he had recently written a very spiritual poem about a bumble bee and, to him, this tiny creature was a definite omen. He knelt down, picked up the tiny bee and held it within the palms of his hands and, without any fear of being stung, he gently blew wafts of air over its body. The tiny bee remained dormant for a little while and then gradually fluttered its wings. Barry then gently raised his arms skywards and, after a few minutes, the graceful creature took to the air. Barry was satisfied now that it had been rejuvenated back to health and able to pollinate more flowers.

I was impressed by his kindness but also aware that we had to press on, as I didn't fancy being stranded on the treacherous mountain.

"Come on our Barry," I encouraged him, "we've a long way to go, we'd better get going or we could be in trouble."

"Don't worry about it our John," he replied quite unaware of any danger, "God will take care of us!"

"I'm sorry Barry, God gave us common sense and that means that we have got to use it to take care of ourselves."

He didn't respond right away but insisted on saying a few prayers before we departed from the spot. Travelling through the wilderness we came across memorials of bygone pilgrims and he insisted on kneeling and saying prayers at each one. Consequently we struggled on and didn't arrive in Roncesvalles until 9 o'clock that night. The albergue was full but luckily we were offered a tent to sleep in. Next day we had to carry on wearing the same dirty clothes that we had worn the day before. Over the next week this was the pattern of things. He insisted on stopping at every little church we passed to pay homage and say a few prayers. Our Barry's intentions were good but the journey was turning into an ordeal and we weren't covering as much ground as we should. Because of his holy habits we had to spend nights sleeping under the stars exposed to the elements.

The pressure was eased a little as we arrived in the village of Los Arcos as it was the 'Paella Festival.' Just like in Pamplona the Spanish were running bulls through the streets. Alleyways were cordoned off and crowds of excited people were roaring loudly.

Unlike the bulls in Pamplona these bulls were much younger and smaller but they were still a force to be reckoned with. To the delight of the spectators many youths ran in front of the bulls and scrambled over the barriers. It was a spectacular event and thankfully none of the locals were hurt. I was thoroughly enjoying the colourful spectacle until I turned around and Barry had vanished. I instinctively knew that he had gone off in search of another church. I felt frustrated as I made my way to an albergue knowing full well that our clothes had yet to be washed. Not only that, the thought went through my mind, did he know which albergue I was in and would he find it before they closed their doors? I loved my younger brother very much but the strain of it all was causing me a lot of stress.

Gradually, thank goodness, our pilgrimage came to an end a week later in the town of Santa Domingo. Barry's spirit was willing but his feet couldn't take any more; they were completely blighted with blisters. Despite the blisters he insisted on going on but I put an end to it saying that I had a chest infection. It was a little white lie, but what else could I do; I think we'd have both collapsed before we reached Santiago. Despite cutting the journey short my younger brother and I still covered 150 miles.

Not to be outdone Barry came out with something else, "Our John, seeing that we haven't completed our Camino, can we help out with the sick in Lourdes?" And so we did and he thoroughly enjoyed working amongst the many disabled people. And just like on the Camino he paid homage to many churches in Lourdes. And it was with my little brother that I actually bathed in the holy waters of the Grotto. Saint Bernadette was to become my favourite saint.

Chapter Seven

Camino Guides

After our Barry's pilgrimage Fred and I got together and talked many times of our footslogging experiences. It was shortly after this that Fred and I were called upon to act as guides on the Camino for fourteen enthusiasts. During the meeting Fred noticed that only seven would-be pilgrims attended the seminar. "Excuse me," he said politely, "but I thought there would be more people here."

Helen, a very pretty young girl replied, "Oh that's because four people have sent in their apologies and three ladies actually live in Spain."

"Live in Spain," queried Fred, "and how do we actually contact them?"

"Oh I've arranged to pick them up at a bus station in Madrid."

Helen was a senior CAFOD worker and she would have overall charge of the group and any expenses involved. She then informed us that, in order to cut down on air pollution and protect the environment, we wouldn't be flying to Spain but would be tavelling overland. "Everyone will meet at St Pancras Station here in London," she asserted, "and from there we will catch a train to Paris. From there we will take an overnight train directly to Madrid. Once we land in Madrid we then have to catch a bus which will take us to our starting point."

"And where will that be?" asked Fred.

"It's a little hamlet near to a mountain village called Ocebriero."

"Oh we know it well," laughed Fred. "John and I have some good memories of that place."

"Oh there's another point Fred," said Helen, "which involves you and John."

"Oh yes, and what's that?"

"Well the train isn't due to land in Madrid until one o'clock and the coach we intend to catch leaves the bus station at ten to two. We're on a really tight schedule as the bus station lies on the other side of the city."

"Don't worry about that, leave it to John, he'll sort it; there's bound to be a taxi rank outside the station."

"By the way," said Helen, "so as to lessen some pressure we've already rang the albergue in Ocebriero and booked a bed for the entire group, and, because everyone will be weary after their pilgrimage, we decided it would be best to fly back to London from Santiago. Is that alright with you two?"

"Yes," replied Fred, "that suits us fine."

"And finally," stressed Helen, "because of the number of people on the pilgrimage, strict health and safety rules apply. Arrangements have been made to hire a car in Spain and employ a driver, as it is compulsory to have a backup vehicle in case of an accident."

"Yeah that seems to make sense," agreed Fred.

On our way back home on the train Fred and I discussed things between us.

"Well it'll be different going on a train instead of flying," said Fred.

"Aye it will, at least we'll be riding through the Channel Tunnel; that's a first for me."

"Yeah, me too; it'll be something to look forward to."

Finally the day of truth arrived. It turned out that John Coppock, a volunteer for CAFOD, was to be our backup driver and his wife drove all three of us to Preston Railway Station. On landing at Euston Station we made our way to St Pancras Station and met up with our future colleagues. Helen was there to meet us and she introduced us to the rest of the group. This was the first time we met up with Ann, a very pleasant bubbly lady from Wrexham. John Foggarty and Tony McNichol gave us a hearty greeting. Other ladies included Sophia, Pat and an African lady from Kenya. Before boarding our train Helen gave each one of us a CAFOD vest to wear on the Camino; and I gave everyone a crucifix. The first part of our journey took us via the Channel Tunnel to Paris where we boarded a night train bound for Madrid. On the journey Fred and I shared a cabin with Tony and John Foggarty and the sleeping arrangements were rather cramped. It was a tedious journey, but this was overcome by breaking open a bottle of wine and a bit of a sing-song. Despite a little tipple it was nigh impossible to sleep that night as the sound of the train wheels going, 'Tat a ta dum, tat a ta dum,' rang in my ears. Likewise the girls shared similar cabins. However, I was told that Pat Downs, a very devout lady, was thrilled to bits as we passed by Avila in Spain with its countless churches.

The tedious train journey finally came to an end as the train came to a stop at Madrid Railway Station. I was well aware that we were on a tight schedule to catch our connecting bus. Picking up my rucksack I sprang onto the platform and dashed to the taxi rank. Luckily I quickly arranged for several taxis to take us to the way out bus station. It was here that Helen hired the backup vehicle for John Coppock to drive and she decided to ride along with him. Luckily the taxis made good time and we arrived with ample time to spare and the ladies, who lived in Spain, were patiently awaiting our arrival. To my surprise one happened to be a nun and her name was Gillian and what a character she turned out to be. From there we all boarded a coach and enjoyed a relaxing ride through miles of open countryside passing many pilgrims along the way. The bus climbed steadily on mountain roads and we actually rode over the magnificent high viaduct near Cacabelos that Fred and I had walked under four years earlier. On reaching our destination we gathered the group together.

"Right ladies and gentleman," said Fred asserting his authority, "we've got a good ten kilometer walk from here to reach our first albergue. We're heading for a small village called Ocebriero and it's a steep uphill climb way to the top of this mountain. It's good really as it'll give you all a chance to stretch your legs before our first long walk tomorrow. And before you set off I want to say something to perk you up on your travels. You will certainly hear it many times along the Way." He then smiled and greeted them with the words, "Buen Camino!"

But before the group set off something rather funny happened. Fred noticed that one very beautiful rich young woman called

Georgina was only wearing a child's rucksack on her back and she was actually carrying a handbag.

"Excuse me miss," he said approaching her, "I don't think it is wise to carry a handbag on the Camino."

"And where will I keep my make-up?" she replied indignantly.

"Your make-up," laughed Fred, "we're not going on a cruise you know, you'd be better off carrying sun cream and mosquito repellant. And, excuse me, where is your rucksack?"

The lady was not amused. "But this is my rucksack," she replied smugly, "I've got everything I need in this one."

"What about a sleeping bag, you can't possibly have one in that small bag?"

"And what do I need a sleeping bag for; I'll be staying in hotels during the walk?"

"You'll be lucky," he laughed, "we're not going on holiday. Anyway, while we're at it, did anyone advise you on what the Camino is about before you set off?" She just ignored the remark looking down her nose at him in disdain. Not everybody had attended our initial CAFOD briefing in London and it was obvious that this lady was one of them. Fred was stuck for words and simply muttered, "Alright madam, suit yourself. All I can say is I hope you're not going to hinder the rest of the group."

It was the beginning of a love-hate relationship.

As Fred and I walked along he was a little riled up. "I don't believe it Juanito, it's the first time that I've ever known a woman to carry a handbag with her on the Camino."

"Never mind Federico, perhaps she'll win you over. You've got to admit she's a good looker."

"Oh aye she's a good looker alright and she knows it. She's also a stuck up bitch. From now on I'm going to call her 'the heiress.'" It was a nickname that was to stick.

I just laughed, "That name suits her mate, but don't forget we're on the Camino."

On the way up the gritty path it became obvious that some of them had not done enough training back home. Surprisingly, Georgina fared very well.

When we arrived at the village it reminded Fred and me of the last time we were here.

"Do you remember us waiting for the albergue to open Federico and hearing Ronnie shouting Johni-i-e-ee?"

"Do I Juanito," he laughed, "how could I ever forget that?"

"And I can well recall having our pilgrim's meal with the Brazilians and meeting up with Peter from Australia who told us about his daughter who'd been into the drug scene."

"Yeah that was a sad story with a happy ending; the magical effects of the Camino certainly worked on that young girl."

On this occasion we didn't have any trouble getting into the albergue because Helen had previously booked the rooms. Mind you, the heiress paid a little extra and had a private room all to herself.

That evening we all sat around a large communal table and Sister Gillian said grace before the meal. Afterwards Fred took charge and addressed the group.

"Right ladies and gentleman this is a good time to get to know each other before we start our Camino tomorrow. However, I just want to point out certain rules. It's important that you don't get lost in the mountains and so here are a few tips. Some of you will be fast walkers and some will be slow walkers. But what you must do is walk at your own pace as it makes it much harder if you try to speed up and likewise, it's very hard to walk slower than your normal pace. Walking on the mountain tracks you will often come to a V junction. So as to guide you there will be a yellow arrow pointing you in the right direction. If you're not sure what to do, just wait there. This is where John and I come into our own. I'm going to spearhead the walk which means no one will be in front of me. John is going to be the 'tail-end-charlie' or back marker if you like. So if you wait where the yellow arrow is, John will eventually reach you. Every now and again I will stop in a village with the support vehicle and wait for everyone to catch up. When John arrives at the village I'll know that every one of you is safe and well." He paused a little before asking, "Any questions?"

"Yeah," replied Tony, "what if we can't find a yellow arrow?"

"Well Tony, like I said if you're unsure which way to go just wait until John catches you up."

It was then that Sister Gillian asked Fred to say the Lord's Prayer' in Spanish.

He declined and handed the chair to me.

Padre nuestro

Que esta's en el cielo

Santificado sea tu nombre

Venga a nosotros tu reino

Hagase tu voluntad

En la tierra como en el cielo

Danos hoy nuestra pan de cada dia

Perdona nuestras offencas

Como tambien nosotros perdonomos

A los que nos offenden

No nos dejes caer en la tentacion

Y libranos del mal……………. AMEN.

After the prayer everyone got together and had a glass of wine or a cool glass of beer…everyone that is except Georgina.

"Oh no thank you!" she declined, "I only drink champagne."

Fred couldn't resist saying, "U-umph, the heiress only drinks champagne does she?"

Once again, she was not amused.

I sensed that the atmosphere was a little frayed so I cut in by giving a toast in Spanish:

"Arriba!"…To the top,

"Abajo!"…The bottom,

"Al Centro!"…The middle,

Y … a Dentro!"…Down the hatch!

Everyone seemed to appreciate the little expression, especially John Foggarty.

Taking everything into account, the day had gone well but Fred and I knew only too well that we were bound to encounter problems in the coming days and one of these would be to get every single person a bed for the night. We hadn't always managed it on our many trips when there were only two of us. To complicate things it was holy year and there were many more pilgrims walking the Camino than Fred or I had ever encountered before.

Next morning after a sparse breakfast we gathered together outside the albergue for a briefing from Fred under a misty atmosphere. After a prayer for the safekeeping of our group Fred addressed them again.

"Right we'll be on our way now," he said emphasizing, "but don't forget what I said about me spearheading the walk and John being the back marker; we don't want anyone to get lost."

Along the Way there must have been a farmer's convention or a fiesta going on in the area as about fifty colourful tractors passed by us. Out came the cameras and many photos were taken including one of a statue of Saint James. The group became engrossed with many more monuments as we passed through small mountain villages. Every now and again we'd come across a fountain where we filled our water bottles. It was an opportunity for me to fill my hat with cold water and put it on my head. This created a laugh amongst the ladies as the water spilled over my face and drenched my clothes.

"You can laugh all you want," I grinned as I recalled what John O'Connor had told me years earlier, "but I'll tell you now, there's no better way of keeping cool along the Way."

After trudging up a steep incline we came across a small hamlet and had a pit stop and a coffee break.

"Enjoy the break," said Fred, "because the next one is a long way off."

Along the Way we had to walk through quaint narrow stone wall gritty passageways where farmers walked their cows ready for milking. It was a tight squeeze and a little frightening as the cows brushed up against us; but they turned out to be rather docile with tiny bells around their necks. Fred and I tended to tease the girls under these circumstances.

"Behave yourselves," Ann would laugh, "it's no wonder they call you the two rascals."

Fred, along with the fast walkers, Tony and John Foggarty arrived at Triacastela, our first stopover at two o'clock and waited there until I arrived with the slow walkers. Luckily there were four albergues and everybody got a bed, albeit in different places. The heiress actually found a private hotel. That night after evening meal we all went to a welcoming mass for pilgrims. A Spanish priest asked for an interpreter and Fred volunteered my services. It was a bit of a let down because when he started talking I could barely understand a word he said.

I was rather embarrassed and so I asked Fred to take over from me.

He just waved his hands in a gesture denoting, "No thank you!"

Surprisingly Gillian offered her services and she translated everything very well.

"I didn't know you spoke Spanish Gillian," I said after the mass had finished. "I feel a bit embarrassed because it's my job on this pilgrimage to translate Spanish."

"Don't worry about it John, you didn't do all that bad," she assured me. "I can only speak a little Spanish but the reason why I could understand him was because he was talking in theological terms and he's from Barcelona. I've served on the altar for many years in Barcelona and it was second nature to me because he was on about the running of the mass."

"Oh that's why I couldn't understand him," I smiled with relief, "he must have been speaking in Catalan."

That night I slept in a large dormitory along with five of the ladies. Out of all of them, Ann was the most efficient. She was a recruiting officer for the Wrens and it stood out a mile. I was up very early next morning but Ann was already in the kitchen and she had coffee and toast awaiting me. This became standard procedure and by the end of our pilgrimage I nicknamed her the 'early bird'. She had a sparkling personality and just laughed at her new tag. All the girls turned out trumps, but I've got to admit that I had a soft spot for Ann.

Taking everything into account, our pilgrimage was going quite well. There were times when the spirit was flagging, but everybody agreed that there was something very special and spiritual about the Camino. Pat especially liked the communal prayers at the start and end of each day's journey. In her own words it helped keep our little flock safe and she always went to bed a happy bunny.

Just as Fred and I had predicted there were times along the Way when there was no room at the inn. At least, there was not room for everyone. This is where the backup vehicle came into its own. John Coppock took four of the blokes to an albergue miles away and then brought them back to the starting point next morning. But on one occasion it caused a bit of a stir as our driver forgot to pick up John Foggarty and fetch him back to the starting point. It was gradually sorted out but it meant that John was hours behind everybody else. Still, he took it in good part and, as he was a good walker, he soon caught up with the rest of the group. One night Pat and Ann were offered accommodation by one of the kind locals. They both got a good night's sleep, but unfortunately they picked up a few extra travellers in their hair.

As the days passed it became evident which pilgrim had trained enough and which one hadn't. A couple of the ladies suffered from blisters and had to ride alongside John in the vehicle. Ann, Helen and Pat fared very well but one day they did something rather naughty. As we passed through a town they decided to slip away from the group and treat themselves to a restaurant meal. That would have been alright, but Fred had carried on and was waiting for me to catch up in the middle of a forest. When I reached him we realised that the three ladies were missing. To complicate matters it started raining heavily. The entire group was getting cold and wanted to move on as the backup vehicle with refreshments was beckoning them in the next village.

"I'll tell you what Federico," I suggested, "you carry on and I'll wait here for them." The rain continued and despite wearing my wet gear I got soaked to the skin and began to shiver with the cold. Finally after about thirty minutes the girls came into sight.

I was too wet and cold to reprimand them and just asked, "Where have you been ladies you know the rule about lagging behind me?"

By the manner in which they responded it was obvious that they'd had an odd glass of wine. "Oh lighten up John; we thought we were entitled to a little treat after all the miles we've walked," they all said in unison.

"That's all very well, but surely you should have considered the rest of the group?"

That's about all I said to them, but when we caught up with the group Fred really tore a strip off them. He let them know in no uncertain terms that he wasn't pleased.

Later along the Way I still felt cold and a little downhearted, but Sister Gillian put an end to that. I caught up with the group at a little inn and she came over and planted a brandy in my hand.

"Here John," she said with a big beaming smile on her face, "get this inside you it'll warm the cockles of your heart."

"But Gillian," I replied a little surprised, "what about the demon drink?"

165

She just roared laughing, "Ha ha, there are times when it's alright my friend and this is one of them. And to prove it I'm having one with you."

I had to smile along with her, "Cheers my friend; buen Camino y vaya con Dios!"

Luckily we all got beds that night and it gave us ample time to dry our clothes. As per usual the heiress booked into a top class hotel. The following day along the Way Fred had a word with her and said that it wasn't in keeping with the spirit of the Camino or with the rest of the group. But it didn't alter things; she actually said, "Who do you think you are; you can't tell me what to do."

Fred was a little annoyed and more or less repeated what he'd just said.

"You're entitled to your opinion," she replied, "but personally I think that every person has to do the pilgrimage in his or her own way. It may seem awful to you that I won't sleep in albergues along with other people but I just couldn't. And it's not that I look down on them, I just can't bring myself to do it. You may not think it

Fred, but I am human and the Camino has touched me a great deal. I feel more humble now than when we first started. It amazes me how the pilgrims are always happy even as their energy ebbs and flows."

"Aye alright," said Fred taken aback, "I'll go along with that. At least I'll give you one thing Georgina, you're a good walker." But he couldn't resist adding with a smile, "But in my book you'll always be the heiress."

She gave a little smile back, "Fair enough, I'll go along with that too."

The little pep talk seemed to clear the air and afterwards Fred and Georgina's relationship became somewhat easier.

The next morning I didn't set off with the group as I wanted to give the slow walkers a head start. As it happened John Fogarty stopped behind with me and we walked along together for two hours. I quite enjoyed walking with him as we exchanged stories of our completely different lifestyles. It turned out that he was a hard worker for CAFOD. Before joining our group he'd previously done other long walks, ran stalls and organised concerts and other social events. He came across to me as a perfectionist in everything he did. But he wasn't stuck up in any way; quite the opposite in fact. He carried a very sophisticated camera and took many interesting photographs along the Way. Gradually we caught up with Helen, Ann and Pat who joined us. Prior to entering a small village we came across a mountain stream.

"Oh look at that," said Ann excitably, "doesn't that water look inviting; how about soaking our feet?"

Every one of us agreed it was a great idea. So it was off with the rucksacks and boots and we all sat and dangled our feet in the refreshing cold water. For the next twenty minutes we laughed and sang like little children; it was great!

"I'll tell you what," said Helen with a big smile on her face, "I love the beauty of this countryside and how the sun seems to fall at different times of the day. U-um, the ambience on the Camino is a total contrast to the streets of London." We all agreed with her sentiments.

Later on that afternoon as we were walking through a small hamlet an old lady approached us offering pancakes and water. Pat was taken aback by the kind offering and couldn't stop talking about it.

That night was the penultimate evening that we would spend together as the following day was our final walk into Compostela and something out of the ordinary happened. We were celebrating outside around a large table when some pilgrims passed.

"Federico y Juanito," one shouted in a strong Spanish accent, "Encantado otra vez mis amigos!" (Pleased to meet you again my friends).

It was none other than Pedro and his wife Maria, whom Fred and I had last seen at the grotto in Lourdes."

I couldn't believe it; it seemed highly coincidental to see them in Lourdes a few years back, but to bump into them again on the Camino; and especially so at this point seemed nigh impossible. The thought instantly went through my mind… is this coincidence or is it fate? I tended to go for the latter.

"Vaya con Dios," said Fred, "you'll have to join us for evening meal!"

So the friendly couple did join our group and another good night was enjoyed by all. Fred and I enjoyed translating as we laughed and conversed during the rest of the evening.

Despite her youth, Helen was extremely efficient and handled tricky situations in a way far beyond her years. However, there were times on the Camino that she felt the pressure of responsibility. And this evening happened to be one of them. It turned out that a couple of the ladies hadn't got a room. Helen became rather frustrated and was almost in tears. The bedroom that Fred, John Coppock and I were in had five beds so we offered to swap rooms. John Coppock wasn't keen on the idea at first as ours was a really cushy room. However, Fred convinced him otherwise that it was no big deal. It solved the problem and took the pressure off Helen. Once again she was back to her own smiling self.

On the walk into Compostela I was again walking with the girls. It was on this last stretch of the journey that once again something special happened. During a respite the girls asked me to tell them of any spiritual events that Fred and I had encountered on our many travels.

I chose to tell them about John Holland, the Irish gentleman who was walking in the footsteps of his sister who, on reaching Compostela, had died in the albergue.

Every one of them agreed it was a very sad tale. But then, just two hours later, as we approached the outskirts of Compostela we came across a memorial which was adorned with flowers. On reading the inscription I couldn't believe my eyes.

It read as follows:

Remember in your prayers

Myra Brennan (52yrs) nee Holland

of Kilkenny and Sligo, Ireland,

who died peacefully in her sleep

in Santiago de Compostela on 24/6/03

having just completed her 2nd consecutive Camino.

"And I shall have some peace there"

"Oh, I don't believe it John," said Ann, "this is the very same lady that you have just been telling us about."

"I can't believe it either" I replied, "the last time we saw John was in Burgos over five years ago." It got me to thinking about life's problems and how everything just seemed to magically slip into place on the Camino.

About thirty minutes later we met up with Fred and the others at a vantage point overlooking the historical city. I mentioned the memorial to Fred and he too was touched.

"Yeah Juanito, I saw it myself, it's unbelievable isn't it? We've always wondered since we left John in Burgos whether he'd made it to Santiago or not."

"Well one thing's for sure Federico; we know now." It was just one more of those uncanny things that tend to crop up on the Camino.

Before entering Santiago we all gathered at the vantage point which gave a fantastic view of the glorious city. At this stage we decided to have a group photograph taken as a memento of the arduous walk. Some young people had erected a small table and were selling bottled water in an attempt to raise money for Latin American children. This put Fred and me in mind of the street children of Brazil.

On reaching Santiago the first place we headed for was the cathedral. We all stayed for the service and once again monks swung the Botafumeiro to a great height dispersing incense throughout the magnificent building. Fred informed the group of the tradition that stemmed from way back in the Middle Ages; and how pilgrims arrived in dirty smelling clothes and the incense was used to overcome the atrocious smell.

Before leaving the cathedral Fred asked me to take a photo of him at a special little altar to take back home to show his family. As it was holy year Fred enlightened the group about a tradition passed down through the ages. According to folklore 'La Puerta Santa' is only opened during a holy year; and if anyone walks through the Holy Door, then all their sins are pardoned. Fred and I had to laugh because, just to make sure, quite a lot of pilgrims walked through it twice.

After the mass the group made their way to pick up their personal Compostela Certificate. They had a rather long wait as hundreds of other pilgrims eagerly queued up to receive theirs.

In Santiago we had no bother booking into an albergue as there were lots of them around the city. One alone had over five hundred beds. Naturally that evening we all gathered together and had a farewell celebratory meal. John Foggarty raised his glass and repeated the words I'd spoken in our first albergue:

"Arriba!

Abajo!

Al centro!

Y ... A dentro!"

Everyone raised their glasses in response. The group thanked Fred and me for our guidance and asked Fred to say a prayer before the meal. And afterwards they persuaded him to give a little speech. The meal was a very special event albeit tinged with sadness as is always the case at the parting of the ways. But before we went our separate ways, Fred asked the group what they had gained from the pilgrimage. The most popular answer was that, despite the aches and pains and little setbacks, life is so different when people congregate together on a spiritual path.

After the meal Fred got a call on his mobile phone regarding something that was going on back home. "Ah well," he said as he put the phone in his pocket, "back to the real world; it looks like I've got a little problem back in blighty."

"But Fred," replied Pat in all sincerity, "to me this is reality, what people are all about; this is the real world. I agree the Camino is tough but it brings out the best and the worst in us. But it tends to fill me with a spirit of complete joy. When I get back home I will always look upon the little yellow arrows as a guiding point in my life."

To Pat's delight the entire group agreed with her sentiments and felt that their ordeal had changed their way of thinking. And to put it in her own words, 'They all went to bed that night happy bunnies'.

The next morning after a thanksgiving prayer we were taken by coach to Santiago Airport to catch our plane for London. And finally on Euston Station we said our goodbyes. Early bird was the last one to greet me; it wasn't like her at all.

Overall the pilgrimage had been a success, and especially so as collectively our group raised over fourteen thousand pounds for CAFOD.

I'd walked the Camino eight times with Fred and I was becoming rather tired as I was now seventy-three years old. Not to be beaten he came up with another idea.

"John I've been thinking of another way of raising money for CAFOD."

"Oh yeah Fred, I hope it's nothing to do with long walks; I don't quite feel up to it anymore."

"No it's to do with a bike ride."

"A bike ride, and where do you hope to cycle to?"

176

"Well you may be surprised, but it came to me in bed last night. I'd like to cycle from CAFOD headquarters in Salford to every other diocese in England and Wales."

"And how do you intend to promote it Fred?"

"Well I've already had a word with CAFOD and they put me in touch with the media boss."

"And what did he come up with?"

"Well he mentioned 'Le Tour de France' and he suggested that it would be a good idea to call it 'Le Tour de Fred'. And he worked it out that it will be over a thousand miles."

"Crikey Fred, a thousand miles, I haven't done any cycling in years."

"That doesn't matter John because what I want you to do is be my backup driver for chance I can't make it."

"For chance you can't make it Fred; how long is it since you rode a bike?"

"Well it's about fifty years," he laughed, "but you know what they say; once you learn to ride a bike you never forget!"

Fred was very persuasive and I would have used my car but then Mark, his son-in-law and an experienced cyclist, offered his services and wanted to cycle along with Fred. He was much younger than us but the gallant man only had one arm. He'd lost it in an accident years earlier serving in the army. He had a camper van which he said could be used as a support vehicle. From that moment on in all weather conditions Fred and Mark were out and about cycling many miles along country lanes to get themselves well prepared for the event. One day I followed them to Blackpool and back to Burnley, a round trip of 90 miles. For practice they did regular hundred mile trips around Lancashire countryside and throughout the Yorkshire Dales. For one exercise I drove them to Morecambe on England's west coast and they both cycled from one side of the country to the other. The narrow country roads through the Yorkshire Dales are renowned for being very hilly and we made just one stopover in Leyburn village. Coincidentally, the name of the small village is an anagram of our own town, Burnley.

On the day of reckoning, with me as their backup driver, they started their crusade from Salford and over five days they covered Leeds, Middlesborough, Newcastle, and Lancaster and finally back to Burnley. In each town we visited schools and churches. Fred used his props in various classrooms and CAFOD named the cause, HUNGRY FOR CHANGE. The children appeared engrossed as he informed them that there are more than 900 million starving people around the world. Each diocese handed Fred a substantial cheque representing money donated by its parishioners. People from each congregation kindly put all three of us up for the night and supplied a supreme evening meal and breakfast.

Sadly, due to unforeseen circumstances I was unable to help them for the rest of the journey which took Fred and Mark to Wales, Somerset, the south coast, London, Birmingham, Nottingham, Sheffield and finally back to Salford. Whilst in Guilford Fred met up with friends from the Camino, Helen, Pat Downs, Anne Coleman and John Foggarty and they cycled with him as far as the Thames Embankment. During the mammoth task, Fred and Mark visited many schools, churches and parishes and talked to more than 3,200 schoolchildren. In various villages many supporters cycled along with them for a few miles to cheer them on in their worthwhile cause. On completing the arduous task Fred and Mark raised thousands of pounds for under privileged people. To their credit, it was a job well done!

When I look back to the time I first met Fred at night school I feel it was fate. He's always been a hard-working man in the building trade. In his own words he's not a rich man, but he's comfortably off. Because of this he feels that he needs to give something back to society. In my book he's certainly done that and much more. If everybody in the world was like Fred … what a wonderful world it would be. He may not be a rich man in money terms, but to me he's rich in human kindness and I feel honoured to have him as my friend.

The following poem is about a pilgrimage in Northern Spain which has been ongoing since the 9th century. Millions of pilgrims from all over the world make the arduous journey year after year.

EL CAMINO DE SANTIAGO DE COMPOSTELA.

'Twas during a course at night school

Students were serious and clannish.

Learning adjectives, verbs and nouns,

Getting to grips with Spanish.

Fred, one of the classmates,

Displayed a festive trend.

During our studying,

He became my special friend.

Part of the course,

In order to obtain a pass,

We'd to talk for fifteen minutes,

In front of the class.

It was a difficult task,

In fact, I found it a pain,

'Cos the speech we had to make,

Was in the language of Spain.

However, a rule of the criteria,

Eased part of the chore,

And gave me the confidence,

To take to the floor.

We could talk about anything,

No matter what the theme,

My task now seemed much easier,

Now, no longer a dream.

My chosen thesis,

Was about different 'Legends in Spain,'

Which in future years to come,

Was to see me trudging in torrential rain.

I became intrigued with 'El Camino de Santiago',

Translated - 'The Road of Saint James',

It jumped right out of the pages,

Like a sparkling ember in the flames.

El Camino de Santiago de Compostela,

A pilgrimage in Northern Spain,

A course, Federico and I,

Traipsed many times o'er stony terrain.

Ongoing since the ninth century,

Renowned the whole world over,

A route o'er Pyrenees Mountains,

Festooned with woods, fern and clover.

Millions of pilgrims take up the challenge,

Each and every year,

Slogging away carrying heavy backpacks',

Smiles on their faces - no sign of fear.

Trudging up many steep mountain paths,

Plodding on in blistering heat,

Aching backs, oozing sweat,

Accompanied with blistered feet.

An average daily walk for the crusaders,

Approximately eighteen to twenty miles per day,

Hopefully reaching an albergue,

A hostel where they can stay.

However, this is not always possible,

As 'Albergue esta completo' by far,

Depicting that the hostel is full,

Only option left - to sleep out under a star.

Federico and I became regular adventurers,

Kitted out in travelling gear,

We became well known on the 'Camino',

Footslogging it year after year.

'CAFOD', a renowned charity,

Accepted Fred and me into one of its bands,

In order to raise sponsor money,

For Third World impoverished lands.

One time we acted as guides,

To a group of fourteen pilgrims or more,

The entire group was inexperienced,

Making it a rather arduous chore.

But the end result was favourable,

After traipsing o'er hills and fells,

Sufficient funds were used in Africa,

To build a new school and water wells.

Compostela derived from Latin, 'Campus Stellae',

Meaning 'Field of the Star',

Many miracles occurred over the ages,

Attracting countless pilgrims from afar.

Pilgrims encouraging each other,

Over muddy and rocky grounds,

Despite being in pain and weary,

Happiness and friendships clearly abound.

If only this planet of ours,

Could liken itself to the 'Camino' free,

Beguiling, so full of love and giving,

What a wonderful world it would be.

Poem about a bumble bee written by my younger brother Barry:

DEUS DIVES MISERICORDIA (God is rich in mercy.)

Thank you little humble bumble bee,

For the thoughts that came to me.

As in church I saw you lay,

On that cold mid-winter's day.

Poor dying, little humble bumble bee,

Why should you have such thanks from me?

'Twas by pure chance I saw you lay,

On the church's aisle that wintry day.

Did you venture out too soon,

Thinking February was June?

Methinks … perhaps you could not wait,

So many flowers to pollinate.

Poor dying, little humble bumble bee so keen,

How sorely tried you must have been.

To see the trees of blossoms bare,

To feel the cruel mid-winter's air.

The church's door was opened wide,

And having found yourself inside.

Cold, hungry and in disarray,

Exhausted on the church aisle you lay.

The creature before the Creator lay,

On that cold February day.

'Twas there we met, perhaps by chance,

But somehow I feel providence.

For now to you I must convey,

That when I first knelt down to pray.

Although I tried hard as can be,

No form of prayer would come to me.

I felt so sorry for you there,

'Twas then my thoughts turned into prayer.

And because of a little humble bumble bee,

'God's Dazzling Mercy' came to me.

My Lord! If a spark of pity can come from me,

For a little humble bumble bee.

How much more, beyond all imagination,

Is the love of God for all His creation.

And I thought upon Jesus' Holy Name,

Formed in a dazzling burning flame.

My risen Saviour from Heaven above,

Ah! So many countless sparks of love.

Ah! Little bee let me explain,

Your brief stay here was not in vain.

Oh no! Your mission in this life was love,

To lift my eyes to my God above.

And it surely was your blessed fate,

No earthly flowers to pollinate.

You did not fail! You reached your goal,

Your pollen touched my very soul.

So thank you little humble bumble bee,

For the hope you brought to me.

I'm glad we met. Ah no 'twas not by chance,

But by Good God's Loving Providence.

Deo Gratias.

Remember in your prayers

Myra Brennan (52yrs) nee Holland

of Kilkenny and Sligo, Ireland,

who died peacefully in her sleep

in Santiago de Compostela on 24/6/03

having just completed her 2nd consecutive Camino.

"And I shall have some peace there."